Table of Contents

IRRESISTIBLE

OBSESSION

DEEPAK GUPTA

Copyright © Deepak Gupta 2024

Embracing Connection: A Special Message to You!

Dear Reader, we are grateful that you are here with your true consciousness along with some high expectations of what value this book will provide for you. We wouldn't tell you why this book is great. *You read it carefully and decide for yourself. That's exactly a good self-help book.* You read and decide whether the techniques will work for you or not. Our one & only request; you should read this book carefully before judging it too early and then you can help yourself by finding novel ways. I have been writing for more than eight years and learned, nothing can make us happy for too long. The cause of happiness today will become the source of sadness but above all, peace can be achieved when we control it entirely in our soul. In this book, we would try making you understand the significance of obsession in your work. ***It's not a book, it's truly my heart. I wrote it in deep solitude from the depths of my heart and soul.***

Our generation perceives enjoyment and work as separate identities but truly they aren't. Most people work and then seek enjoyment while some people enjoy deeply while enjoying the process of their work deeply. What most people suggests; do the hard work but it creates pressure in my heart. ***IRRESISTIBLE OBSESSION***, the book will possibly guide you to perceive work a smooth play, so you don't have to work your entire life. You just have to play. When everything goes against us, we try doing the hard work but it's actually not required. It's something else. Read the book slowly & carefully to find out!

To travel far, there is no better ship than a book. - Emily Dickinson.

I Can't Thank You Enough! I'm so Grateful!

Deepak Gupta.

Prologue: Discipline is Exaggerated

To the experts, what looks like hard work from the outside is play from the inside. - Naval Ravikant.

Discipline is overrated. It feels tough, powered & pressured on our routine while true obsession is underrated. Obsession is merely a play, a great pleasurable play from our heart & soul. It doesn't need any perfect routine. Our entire life is dedicated to it unknowingly. Meanwhile, discipline is visible with time but obsession makes time invisible. Obsession may not be the best of the world but can give you the best feeling of the world.

Diogenes once said, there is a false love that will make you something you are not. Suppose you were the last person on earth, who would you impress? Of course, there would be no one to impress but yourself. If you don't ever find anyone to impress, impress yourself intensely. Now, you can perceive yourself like Diogenes as the last person on earth who never cared for what people think of him. It's not a criticism but an appreciation for him. ***May be many people aren't aware of the Diogenes of Sinope who was insulted with the name doggish as he thought dogs as the most honest.*** He was so honest that he often did masturbation in front of the public and depicted, I hope I could fulfil my hunger just by rubbing the belly too. It may seem an act of foolishness but it's damn true we are guided by some invisible pressure, society morals, and subconscious thoughts; & even without knowing, we are prioritizing the entire world before ourselves. If you aren't still aware of Diogenes then for sure, you are very well aware of **Alexander the Great**. Who can forget the personality who had won almost the entire world and still felt restless! Can you now think of the invisible border where there was a man Diogenes who had nothing and never cared for anyone's thoughts and opinions and on the other side, we had, Alexander the Great, who had everything, the world's best fortune.

There's an extremely interesting famous tale of Alexander the Great and Diogenes where Alexander encountered him for the first time and it's merely a play but touched the hearts of the universe.

Alexander the Great: Do you need any favours from me?

Diogenes: Yes, stand out of my sunlight!

Alexander the Great: If I were not Alexander then I wish to be Diogenes.

Diogenes: If I were not Diogenes, I should also wish to be Diogenes.

The above depicted play is merely astounding where both the honest men were damn satisfied with what they were doing.

They were not forced but interested. History clarified, Diogenes often begged for a living and slept in a large ceramic jar with honesty. He used his simple life to criticize the corrupted and confused society. He had also done some philosophical stunts where he was carrying a lighted lantern in broad daylight, claiming to be looking for an honest man. Diogenes clarified all the lessons of an honest life by living one in which wisdom, happiness and peace belong to the man who is independent of society. *Maybe you want to win the entire world or to be yourself. That's the choices of our souls.*

We know, obsession feels negative, a very negative approach & discipline looks good but really overrated. Right? Discipline is purely forced and it tells you to be tough on yourself just merely by its existence. If you often tell yourself to be disciplined then you aren't devoting yourself to the work entirely. It's like suggesting a sad man to be happy. ***What if I say to you, stop being sad, when you are sad? So, I can't say to myself to be disciplined forcefully when I'm in my comfort zone.*** If work is play, we should enjoy and devote every moment to it with fullness but in between we aren't running towards our work but getting pushed. There's a vast difference. ***Obsession pulls us towards the work. Discipline pushes us to do anything.*** So, if ever in life, you often have to say to yourself to be disciplined, you aren't doing entirely what you love from your soul.

I'm writing this book and I'm damn sure, I was restless this morning to penned down my ideas. I was getting pulled from my home to the office. Obsession feels negative but it gives you the best satisfaction of this world, not for others but yourself. ***Really, if you seek it you can't ever find it.*** If you seek discipline as a visible force, you can only focus on it but when you are getting pulled out of the universe to do your loving work, you will not force yourself but ultimately stop yourself from doing the work. You will forget the feel of time, fly in the air, dance on the clouds and dedicate every cell to your loving work without even knowing the pressure of becoming disciplined.

As we clarified, Diogenes felt dogs were honest & even he was insulted with the name doggish. Dogs usually eat, make love in public, go barefoot, & sleep on roads. They are shameless animals, not as being beneath modesty, but as superior to it. They are good guard and often distinguish between friends and enemies. After all, Diogenes taught us self-sufficiency for happiness and also the shamelessness of what we want; a life of true honesty dedicated to our soul.

Why I chose to write this book! Before I would clarify the exact reason to you, primarily, I asked myself the same question because strong reasons are very significant to go forward. During my career of writing many good and bad books, I have criticized myself more than anyone else because I was never satisfied with what I was writing. That was my first doubt within my soul. I had miserably failed in initial few years but I was still improving, understanding and writing continuously even without caring whether the readers would read my books or not. I'm not being self-obsessed but analysing myself so that I don't even have to halt my writing when I would get nothing from this world. It was for me, only me, the vision only I was perceiving in my soul. That may seem tough to the world but you know, I'm self-fulfilled, accomplished, happy and in peace. Now, the question is how it can be possible. I was disciplined even without knowing it. When I asked myself what discipline is, I found my answer, it's bullshit. It's nothing. Its void. Discipline can be a beginning to a good thing but it would vanish away as soon as your interests get dull with time. In this world, where everyone is choosing the best, a rare people are choosing what they really want for their soul. Of course, if you want to seek the best and you don't love it, surely, you have to force yourself towards that work and do the hard work but my friend, hard work doesn't build history. It's pure love.

Now, how this book will ever assist you to become the person for your true soul. *Irresistible Obsession, the book has carefully crafted thirty well researched practical techniques for automatic discipline without much efforts & pain, skill mastery and work obsession to control your fortune. This book is insanely deep to aid you to find your own soul and the minute details of your most loving work. It's a pure treasure for artists, routine work, painters, workaholic people, businessman, & writers; Ultimately, for creative & passionate people who want to live a fulfilled life. With techniques from the history, the book, Irresistible Obsession will transform your life forever while making you into the person who can reach and accomplish his goals intensely with deep perfection, without any hurry along with taking proper rest & peace. In gist, it will bring out your best flawlessly even without giving any pain to do it.*

As discipline is forced, it's short term and you have to continuously remind yourself that you are missing something. ***Meanwhile a true discipline comes without any factors but comes with a purpose.*** When we force ourselves to work, we build less resilience that even a small discomfort can make us lethargic & distract from our purpose. That's why we hold the high resilience of failure in the work we truly love and that builds the great obsession or you can say true discipline in the work you honestly worship. In gist, don't chase discipline but everything else. It's usually the endless efforts of many combined factors. Perceiving discipline as a sole factor to do world class work is bullshit. A true discipline comes in its absence, when we get lost in something & we would never know whether we were disciplined or not and that's why discipline is overrated. It forces you to become what you aren't. We are seeking a true path where you would love to walk, so you wouldn't feel the pebbles, problems and tiredness while reaching there, it's ultimately the enchanting view, peaceful journey and endless love.

Discipline is darkness. Obsession is light. There's an *astounding tale of an old* man who was living his life in absolute darkness. He never knew what the power of light was but still he was damn contended in the dark. Even if it was painful, dark and forced, he thought life was like that. It's same as the tough discipline but one day, he saw the point of light in a direction very far from him. That light was an obsession. It was his passion. He was loving it with his heart and started running towards it. What he was feeling painful in the dark, now running in the same darkness peacefully because he wanted that bright light because he loved it. Now, that darkness was killing him more and he wanted to remove or possibly reduce the darkness. It's absolutely true, until we are in complete darkness, everything is okay. We behave and get habitual to live like that but as soon as we experience the light, we start to know the depth of the darkness & that's the true difference between obsession and discipline. Discipline forces you to run in the dark endlessly, obsession pulls you to something you love, that builds your high energy in the dark, even if there was nothing changed in the dark. It's the same darkness but now you are seeing the loving light. That light changed everything, not the darkness. Always try to do the most intense dance while you are doing something from your heart & then you will realise, the entire world is fixed and placed wrongly to seek the best. The right people for the wrong tasks takes more stress & pain to earn their livelihood.

The most intense people weren't focused on being disciplined but on their obsession & that becomes irresistible as soon as they cherish it. If you aren't doing what you really love, what else you can expect from discipline. It's like a strong rope is given to an elephant to do the skipping. Discipline is definitely overrated. It's purely forced on our souls and we feel, we don't have to force ourselves to do our best. We just have to be ourselves. We need something so that we can get pulled towards the view instead of running endlessly to know what we would get in the end. To do the passionate dance, you have to love it intensely.

As we elaborated early, ***Diogenes was a true cynic and also the founder of cynicism.*** A cynic is a person who believes people only do things for themselves rather than to help others. Diogenes was the most fascinating & honest person of the history. Also, Alfred Hitchcock is the master director who understood the master of visual storytelling and he clarified, ***'The best actor for a part is the one who can do it without acting.'*** And I can say it's definitely deep and a masterpiece quote that tells us to be ourselves and natural. We can't be good if we force something on ourselves but we would become best or even great along with satisfaction when we choose to be ourselves; just ourselves.

It's often said, discipline is painful but it's painful when we force ourselves to do something that doesn't belong to us or we don't love it actually, otherwise when we do something with our heart, we become irresistibly attracted, passionate & obsessed with our loving work forever.

One of the huge mistakes people make is that they try to force an interest on themselves. You don't choose your passion; your passion chooses you. - Jeff Bezos.

Strategy 1

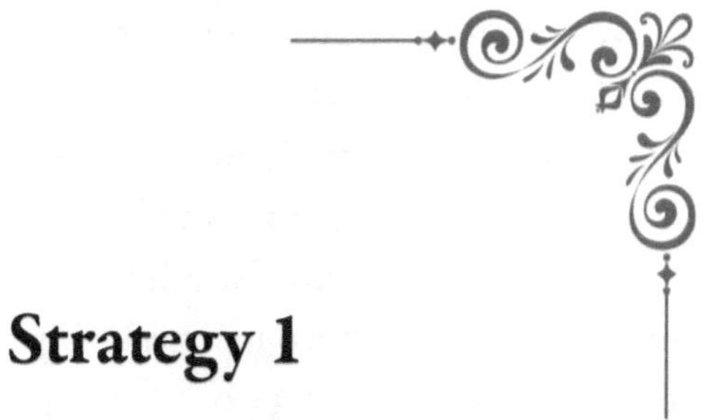

Focus is Pure Obsession: Pablo Picasso and Vincent Van Gogh Strategies for Creating MASTERPIECES

Don't bend, don't water it down; don't try to make it logical; don't edit your soul according to fashion. Rather follow your most intense obsessions mercilessly. - Franz Kafka.

Focus is meditation. Multitasking is overrated. I usually feel more energetic when I focus. Also, even after work, I don't feel exhausted but tremendously energetic to move the mountain even after the work accomplishment.

Franz Kafka once depicted, **'Writing is a sweet, wonderful reward and a non-writing writer is a monster counting insanity.'** And even when he considered his own life after writing, he penned, I don't want peace for writing like a hermit, that wouldn't be enough but like a dead man. We feel the words of Franz Kafka and understand how focused and gloomed he was when he was writing his letters to his father, **Hermann Kafka** and lover **Milena Jesenska.**

When I thought, I had to focus well, I was so distracted by this world. When I was forcing myself to look into my loving work too hard, I was entirely distracted with anything and lost my mind in the end. That's so bizarre. So, if I'm loving my work, why do I have to force myself to do my best work. I can naturally focus for long without getting exhausted any more. Focus is purely meditation whether you do it deliberately to calm your mind or doing something you truly love. When we don't force our mind and heart to do something, we are purely free from utilising our energy too much. That's magic.

While doing something you love, you can be hyper active, hyper productive, hyper focused and produce the best output of your life and even without feeling too much pressure on your mind because now you aren't forcing yourself to focus but something else that brings it automatically to you. That's enchanting. So, instead of forcing myself to do something and finding focus, I would rather choose where I don't have to find focus. Obsession can be created when you don't bother about its result but the process. The honest process can make you feel too lost that you don't even bother too much about the result, anyway. *If you feel good while doing it, you are purely doing something equivalent to mediation.*

Now, when people say I'm finding focus, I feel gloomy for them because you don't have to find discipline or focus but yourself and interesting learning is, you will be more focused, disciplined and extremely obsessed in your loving work without even knowing it.

Vincent Van Gogh, a master and most popular post-impressionist painter wasn't widely appreciated during his entire life. He crafted almost *2100 artworks including around*

860 oil paintings & most of them in the last two years of his life after when he almost took his own life while shot himself with a revolver in the wheat field & died two days later. He lived his life in such extreme poverty that he didn't have canvas to paint, so history tells, he had painted a lot on his paintings and God knows, how much masterpieces are still under these masterpieces. Vincent Van Gogh even created one of the most expensive masterpieces **Starry Night in The Saint Paul de Mausole Asylum in France.** Those days he was admitted to a hospital due to mental illness. Sometimes there's a misinterpretation between madness and obsession but it's true, when you are mad about something, then you can create the world's best MASTERPIECE. Vincent Van Gogh is widely appreciated for his expressive paintings with energetic application and emotive use of brilliant colours. Now, I think he didn't even get wealth in his entire life but while creating it, so how focused, honest and passionate he was actually. *That focus is pure obsession and I felt he never forced himself but purely natural while playing with his paintings and that's how true masterpieces are created.* It's astounding to know, he created a new work every 36 hours. **Can you imagine a world class painting in 36 hours?** And if you are feeling astonished with it then *Pablo Picasso is the great master of his field.* Now what I would write ahead will make you feel uneasy, Vincent Van Gogh never started painting until he was 27 years old & never got any formal training. Affirmative, he was self-taught. It was all natural and he was truly loving it, that's it. Do you think he was ever aware of feeling more focused as he wasn't getting anything monetary out of it?

So, if you are still seeking focus, you aren't doing what you want. ***You don't have to chase anything, nor do you have to force yourself, just find what you are passionate about and you are in the club of Irresistible Obsession.***

Until you are mad about something or someone, you don't truly love it. You have to choose it for every moment even if the entire world is on fire or the sky collapses because that's what true love is.

Pablo Picasso once said, ***'Inspiration exists, but it has to find you working.'*** Almost every well aware citizen of this world is widely aware of the world's most energetic and masterclass painter, ***Pablo Picasso***. He lived for a total of **33,403 days** and created **26,075 published works** from age 20 until his death at the age of 91. We feel focus has a direct relationship with the longevity of your life too because when you are automatically focused, you forget every pain, distraction, problems and stress. It relieves your stress and makes your organs healthier for a long time. *Can you imagine the focus of Pablo Picasso who created something new every day for 71 years?* Can you say it forced? Absolutely not, he was loving it than caring about any focus or discipline. Discipline is purely forced power that tries to make you something you aren't and if you're taking pain in the process then what's the use of the result. Try to feel pleasure in the process and you will forget about the result even if you get the world's best. You will return to your work for that irresistible pleasure in the process. Meanwhile, Pablo Picasso entirely created 50,000 works of art, almost *2 per day* but if we include the total artworks, it was massively ***1,47,800 pieces including 13,500 paintings, 1,00,000 imprints and 300 sculptures and ceramics with***

3400 illustrations too. That's an impressive & highly productive 78 years career ever.

At last, Pablo Picasso is the real-life instance of a brilliant man with a deep focus on his professional painting career. If you are entirely focused on what you love, you feel less exhausted and even get more focused than you are seeking. Others may feel your obsession as an insane work schedule but it's extremely normal for someone who is loving it with a heart and not feeling hard while accomplishing it.

I put my heart & soul into my work, and I have lost my mind in the process. - Vincent Van Gogh, A Post-Impressionist Dutch Painter.

Seek your true loving work. Focus is purely meditation. Multitasking is overrated. It confuses the mind and reduces creativity & productivity.

There are some days when I think I'm going to die from the overdose of satisfaction. - Salvador Dali, a World Class Painter.

An ounce of action is worth more than a ton of theory. - Ralph Waldo Emerson.

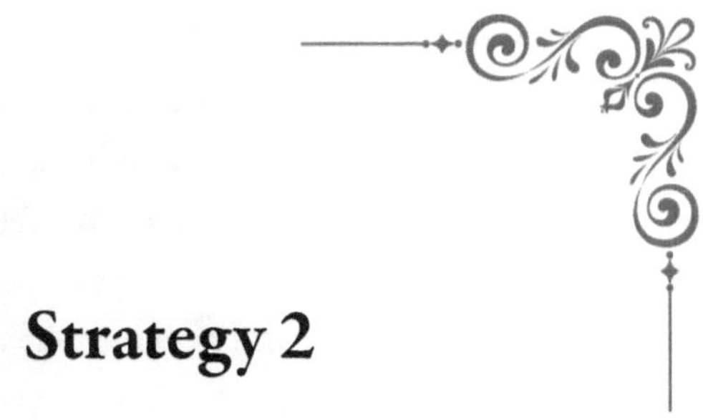

Strategy 2

Great Everyday Fortune: How to Seize Your Entire Day and Build an Unbeatable Ritual for Eternity - Taste the Pleasure of Good Habits

To move the world, we must move ourselves. - Socrates.

Nikola Tesla died at the age of 86. Charlie Chaplin died at the age of 88. Pablo Picasso died at the age of 91 but Vincent Van Gogh died at the age of 37 years in which he shot himself out of mental turmoil and mentioned, 'Sadness will last forever.' In history, there were certain workaholic people like Vincent Can Gogh, Pablo Picasso, Mother Teresa, Michael Jackson and Marie Curie in which some lived miserably but created the best masterpieces of all time. Building a great everyday fortune requires a high level of consciousness to understand our own character first. We have read many articles, research papers and books to know what actually fascinates the entire world and how they can also make any day a perfect day for both work and pleasure and at last, we found, there's no one. ***Yes, we found no perfect routine.*** When we thought mornings are best to work insanely, some great artists like Pablo Picasso woke up at 11'o clock in the morning and still thrilled the entire universe with their creations. There are always good exceptions for a perfect routine and it's totally reflected in our nature and nurture. With diverse interests, routines, & environment, we finally have concluded, a great day is directed by the extreme balance of both obsessed work and deep pleasure and both are interlinked. If you aren't happy in personal life, you may not get the best output while working. And if you aren't happy with your work, you may mess up your personal life. Whether you are the world's wealthiest person or a workaholic or an idle person, you always need a dynamic routine along with exceptions to make it close to relevant and dynamic to make it interesting.

After scrounging history, personalities lives, struggles, opinions, articles, research, unbiased observations and books, we have found three phases that conclude the entire day of humans:

A. Great Morning Fortune: Research says, every human should be an early riser. We all should wake up before the sunrise and stay calm in our morning schedule. I even consider doing the easiest task in the morning and wander like I'm the most unemployed person on this planet. Now, here comes the dynamics. Some people want to wake up early and attack the work as they get enough energy while some try to be on hibernation mode and save their energy for the entire day. The required amount of energy depends on the nature of work you are doing. Apart from all debates, there's also a kind of nature's clock that is far essential to keep the body, soul, mind and heart in a true coordination. Maybe you have a great body but your mind is exhausted and vice versa. Be well aware of everything.

When it comes to following nature's call, Japanese people are far ahead of this world and after researching I found a most popular *Japanese writer Haruki Murakami*, writer of the most popular book of *Norwegian Woods* who wrote, *'What happens when people open their hearts? They get better.'* We are really fascinated by his simple routine and we can call it the best routine ever if you want to follow the power given by nature. Haruki Murakami wakes up at 4am even though without any alarm because he falls asleep at exactly 9pm, totalling to give him seven hours of sound sleep. When we follow nature's routine, we feel less tired and thus need less sleep too. The more we oppose nature's routine, the more exhausted we can be and therefore need more rest. After being awake up at 4am, he straight works for 5-6 hours continuously i.e. directly attacked the artistic writing. That's a long duration of writing process. In the afternoon, he goes for 10km running or 1500m swimming which he finds convenient. After that in the evening, he reads a bit & listens to some music and at 9'o clock night, he falls asleep with lights off. Now, there can be certain debates for this routine because he's missing the social life, household chores, family time and friends but as he's extremely satisfied in it, it can well contribute to the best routine for Haruki Murakami. It can be a great learning experience to follow nature's call.

After analysing the morning routines of successful people, I found some had tremendous energy as soon as they woke up but some created energy after they woke up. Likewise, if we dig deep into the morning schedule of **Martin Luther King Jr**, he usually woke up at 6am and started his day with prayer, meditation and radiating positive energy into his soul. We recommend, don't start your day with negativity, burden, pressure, force or any kind of stress because it would consume your good energy and can make you tired even before the end of the day instead start your day well and it can be peaceful and neutral to save your energy for the entre day.

While ***Haruki Murakami*** attacks the work as soon as he wakes up, ***Jeff Bezos***, the world's wealthiest man feels, quiet mornings are very significant for the entire day productivity. He takes eight hours of sleep every day and goes to bed early and gets up early. At least that's also close to nature's call to admire its beauty. Even when I was traveling the different cities of India, I realized, the true beauty of God can be enjoyed to learn the art of being an early riser. As soon as Jeff Bezos wakes up, he brews some coffee, reads the newspaper and generally does not start his work, a very different mindset. He even usually cooks breakfast for his kids, sometimes pancakes and he even do the dishes. ***It's the Jeff Bezos idea of Puttering.***

Puttering depicts doing things or tasks in a relaxed way, without forcing ourselves an inch, without trying very hard for them. Jeff Bezos even said, puttering time is very essential for him and that's why he likes to do the dishes, listen to music, and make breakfast. Basically, puttering gives relaxation & peaceful breaks to slow down our minds.

According to a study by ***Biologist Christoph Randler***, ***people who do great performance in the morning time are better positioned in career and success*** because they are more proactive than people who are at their best in the evening. Put differently, your morning productivity, alertness and energy is far better than doing the same tasks in the evening.

Now, if we consider the world's best literature writers of the history of all time, ***William Shakespeare***, he usually woke up at 4:45am to take advantage of the natural light. I have also worked straight for long hours in the natural light t& have understood, it's best for productivity, makes you feel alert, more energetic and away from stress. As soon as William Shakespeare woke up, he got straight to work at 5am. It may be noted that, it's not much significant that you are an early riser but significant is what you do as soon as you wake up. After analysing we found, some people straight get to the work to utilise their initial energy while some put themselves in hibernation mode to save energy for the entire day but in total, they all are energetic when they work. So, are you utilizing your first energy in the work you love or you are getting exhausted even before reaching there? You should have the right energy to follow your passion.

History says; now expanding PP routine, ***Pablo Picasso is the most productive artist ever*** and what interesting is, he woke up at 11 in the morning. Here most of our myths get busted but in between, he had the long hours of uninterrupted work that allowed him to be hyper creative and productive. Pablo Picasso fell asleep from 3am to 11am, then after 11am to 2pm, he preferred breakfast and some leisure time with friends & family. After, he came in his most productive mode from

2pm to 10pm, he painted continuously and then 10pm dinner and usually people sleep at such time but he also decided to work from 11pm to 3am, that's aggressive schedule. I can feel the tiredness if someone follows his routine and you doesn't love his work. As he loved his work till the last day, it would be so natural for him that he felt extremely energetic and satisfied while doing it. It's all about perspective and love.

Finally, can I give you the best secret of your life on productivity, it's not about where you are giving your time but where you are utilising your energy, that's what matters. Time is an illusion to get fit into the schedule. If you want **MASTERPIECE** of your life, take care of your high energy, otherwise when you reach to accomplish your most loving work, you may fail because you wouldn't have the sufficient energy even if you want to accomplish it.

Painting is just another way of keeping a diary. - Pablo Picasso.

Do you keep a diary in any form of art where you can see yourself, where you can understand yourself truly?

B. Work Obsession: The kind of work you do and the energy you put into your work will decide what kind of peace and love you will get in the night. As we feel, the entire day & night is interlinked. If you aren't cautious in the morning, you will get exhausted before the arrival of your loving work. So, it's like hitting the right energy at the right time to the right work to get the best outcomes and decisions. We learned, some great personalities start their work at 4am while some at 11am and surprising fact is, whether they save their energy till that time or create more energy through their routine but at last they get lost into their deep and right work to lost the track of the time. Here we are counting the time of every productive personality but they never looked at time but the true focus and sufficient energy. They worked till they found themselves active and as soon as they get exhausted, they slowed down and took reasonable rest too.

As many great personalities don't have the exact time of work but researchers found the best brain sharpest time is in the morning from 10am to 2pm and after that 4pm to 10pm. They consider 2pm to 4pm extremely slow for doing the creative work. Apart from everything else, what's the most underrated thing in work is the reasonable rest. It's extremely normal, when you are highly energetic, you cease to slow down and sometimes go beyond everything to accomplish your work but in the long run, it exhausts us and hampers the productivity itself. If you are working non-stop even for the work you love, you may feel exhausted and then it may bring stress to the word ultimately. People sometimes blame too much work but they never bother to take the right naps in between to restore their energy. Even Albert Einstein usually slept ten hours a day and he recommended to take short naps during the day for high level of mental alertness & hyper productive state.

Naps are purely underrated in any work schedule. It may feel like we are wasting time but indirectly it adds us to the best energetic state. Sacrificing or you may say, investing such time can put us into the best mental & creative state too.

Uberman Sleep Cycle recommends a combination of six 20 minutes naps spaced evenly throughout the day and 3 hours of sleeping during the night, totalling 5 hours of sleep a day but that's extremely difficult to implement even in hyper productive state. I have read some people's opinions on following such a routine but in the long run, it's disastrous, so we don't recommend it for healthy living. Most people avoid their health while chasing their dreams but it's the balance that can take you far.

We have to go far happily than to go fast sadly.

Also, there's a **Slumber with a Key Method** to take a perfect nap during the work hours. It's the famous technique of most famous painter **Salvador Dali** who used it very often to bring out the best creativity and energy out of his soul. The technique suggests us sleeping on a chair while holding a pair of keys or a spoon that can create loud noises. While sleeping, once our consciousness is lost, our arms will eventually leave the object on the floor. The sound of this hitting the floor should be loud enough to wake you up. Salvador Dali said, as soon as he woke up after this state, the measured rest had improved his creativity. Also, this nap will remain for less than an hour which provides you with the best of both awake and sleep positions.

A great work is guided by great focus. Focused people are happy and live longer.

You can conclude any work in relevant time but producing the best work of your life requires the best details. The more perfect you are, the great masterpieces of your result will be.

Can you bring back the time you have passed on regret?

C. Deep Peaceful Nights: It's the most debatable topic in human lives. At night, some love to sleep peacefully in their cosy beds while some love to stay awake and follow their passion mercilessly.

Although, the **National Sleep Foundation** recommends the great way to get a peaceful sleep is first getting into a state of calm which will help you fall asleep. If you want to sleep like a baby, you have to be carefree like a baby, doing the calm things on this planet before you fall asleep.

Bill Gates said, I read an hour almost every night. It's part of falling asleep. He also told the Seattle Times, finishing the day by reading will help you to become a cultivated person.

At night, we prefer you to be inclined towards love than obsession. Obsession of work can be followed but without balance, after a few days you may feel something is making you uneasy but there's another real-life successful instance of Pablo Picasso, Vincent Van Gogh, Nikola Tesla and Franz Kafka who preferred to work at night in hyperactive mode and got highly successful. It's highly debatable.

Research says, *Artists work better at night due to audio visual calmness.* Sound and light can be overstimulating for artists. At night, the world becomes a softer place when it comes to sound and light. Meanwhile, I'm also the person who tries to find out peaceful place to write than the most beautiful. It's our priorities.

Also, I read it somewhere and I loved it as an artist, no one looks back on their life and remembers the nights they had plenty of sleep.

Franz Kafka when he was frustrated with his living quarters and day job, wrote in a letter to Felice Bauer in 1912, '"time is short", my strength is limited, the office is a horror, the apartment is noisy & its a pleasant straightforward life is not possible then one must try to wriggle through by subtle manoeuvres.'

Vincent Van Gogh said beautifully, 'I often think that the night is more alive and more richly coloured than the day.'

Strategy 3

The Power of Slowing Down & Taking Good Rest: Unleashing Your True Potential to Take Reasonable Rest & Energize Yourself

Wisely and slowly, they stumble that run fast. - William Shakespeare.

A most popular and truthful American Novelist & short story writer **Ernest Hemingway** said, *'The important thing is to have good water in the well and it is better to take a regular amount out than to pump the well dry and wait for it to refill.'*

We should grow with work but not get consumed.

As soon as we get conscious in life, we all want to achieve the greatest and best as fast as possible. Apart from everything, we all desire to become wealthy overnight but for what, to sleep peacefully and without any stress but of course, we can still do it right now when we have enough for this life. Put all together, it's our own desires to get more and then we become obsessed with what we want. There's nothing wrong with it going fast in life but it can't take us far. *In the above message, Hemingway elaborated the power of slowing down and taking a deep rest to refill our souls.* If we are always utilizing too much of our energy then when we would get time to refill it. Whether it's a Salvador Dali Technique to take a power nap on the chair with slumber with a key method or Bill Gates to read more and more books every day to learn more, we all have to slow down to restore our souls.

Young bloods often run fast to achieve their dreams but forget when they are young, they also have to enjoy the world too. Salvador believed, after taking the perfect nap, the rest had improved his creativity. ***Remember you prayed for today, so for being worried?*** Slowing down is a technique to think for your soul, to understand whether you are getting fulfilled with what you are doing or not. Your passion isn't for being too hurry. We believe every work is a work of art. If you aren't enjoying it then you will feel pain for it the entire life. Enjoy today as well along with doing your best. I'm repeating, remember you prayed for a good today? And Now you are here. Enjoy well.

Now, taking a right pause, slowing down and taking a good rest is purely an art. Today's generation wants to go fast but in ancient times, our ancestors were enjoying every moment by focusing well on their work. If they were hunting then they were hunting solely and what they were constantly getting was the pure social interaction. ***We don't have more pain now but a less people who would understand our pain.*** In negative solitude, we are getting consumed. Here, slowing down and taking a good rest means to enrich your soul with or without people. We have to involve ourselves in activities that don't consume us but make us feel soothing & energetic in the long run. Now, at most tasks, we are getting consumed. When we seek rest, we aren't taking rest but getting more consumed even more than our work and that's why people are tensed, stressed and depressed. They are slowing down & taking a rest but not getting energized for their work. Our generation is more mentally exhausted because we are much involved in going fast, using the internet very frequently and not thinking for ourselves. I have realized, people are chilling on the internet for their fun and then calling is rest & enjoyment. ***If you are taking a rest and still not getting energized, you are taking the wrong rest.*** Our work concepts are bit debatable because we have a concept of getting exhausted physically and mentally but in the right work, you would get less physically exhausted but get mentally energized, and that's why some people are very happy while some are sad because they don't know they are employed in the wrong areas of their lives.

Can you believe focused people live longer? That's debatable but affirmative, they can because such people use less senses while accomplishing a work and divert their mind from problems to a particular work while a multitasker or divergent mind train themselves to do many tasks at a time and may get involved in stress and problems when occurred.

If you aren't well convinced let me give you some true research facts:

- Japanese people live longer because they develop strong social relationships, love and friendships even with their strong life purpose.

- I found Pablo Picasso lived longer because he was truly focused on his passion and followed a simple routine enjoying both professional and personal life because he had a strong life purpose. Purpose is damn significant for longevity.

- ***Most people are depressed because they aren't happy with what they are doing.*** Out of control factors can be out of control but what you can control is your life satisfaction from your work but most people aren't utilizing it. You know, Depression leads to 67% increased risk of death from heart disease & 50% increase in the risk of death from cancer.

- In Great Morning Fortune, Herbal Tea, Flowers Tea, Black, White and Green Teas are Japanese people's routine. I even experienced, people who live near mountain areas or even **Azerbaijan** people drink herbal teas to make themselves active & healthy. Now a day, we are consuming more processed & inorganic foods that aren't making us feel good.

- *Peace and calm are very cheap yet costly these days* because we have made it too far from ourselves by our own choice. Focused people are peaceful because they aren't getting consumed with time even when they are alone.

- *How mentally well you are but if you aren't physically fit, you may feel tumult or discomfort in everyday life.* You may feel lethargic or even less active with your true potential which can hamper your mental status as well. It's the true rule of Japanese and ancient people to stay mentally, physically, emotionally & spiritually active.

- ***I have found, healthy people don't have experimental routine.*** They get stuck to a straightforward good routine with only little dynamics. They try hard finding their sense of satisfaction from various tasks and implement them consciously into their lives. They even consider simple & better hygienic nutrition but not the fancy ones.

- **Japanese people are mostly goal-oriented people** & that's why they live longer because they don't have time focusing more on problems but shift their minds to better opportunities. They manage their stress, calm their minds and often change their mindset to explore more.

- How much pain you are giving to your body every moment really matters a lot. There are people who are crying while carrying out their work while some are enjoying their work. That's what make the big difference. *If you are loving, you will do more than required but if you are crying you will accomplish less than you want. That makes a great difference.*

- Solitude is really a significant art of living in our own way. *Most people are afraid of being alone because they don't know what to do when they are all alone.* If you feel bored when you are alone then you are boring. If you can't entertain yourself, you can't entertain anyone. The source of solitude and enjoyment should be within our heart, not in someone else's heart. Solitude gives you the chance to explore your bad areas of interest & gives us consciousness and constant motivation to improve them.

- There's a *Japanese Hara Hachi Bun Me* rule that depicts us to *stop eating when we are 80% full*. A proverb also suggests us to eat our food like medicine otherwise one day we have to eat medicines like food. The right amount of food in our belly makes us feel alert, active and confident. Hara Hachi Bu for longevity prefer us to take long walks, stay calm, take a balanced diet and focus on our goal that makes us happy. So simple as that. To achieve such a life, reduce your desires and you are already there.

- When you slow down, you give a great chance to explore your work once again with more alertness and that can give you a best shot with deep intensity. Even artists utilise it very well. Most writers write slowly to let their feelings come out from their hearts as deeply as they can.

Slowing down is a technique. Taking a good rest is purely an art. It doesn't mean to make ourselves into a sleepy position but we have to think about mental, emotional, physical and spiritual rest. That's a true good rest. If you are sleeping well, you are giving rest to your physique only. Hence, first we should be well aware of a great combination of a good rest. You know, what's the best habit in the world, to read a good book again & again. Steve Jobs, Bill Gates, Jeff Bezos, Elon Musk or even the most peaceful people of the century read books every day. Before they go to sleep, they prefer a good book to read as they feel it's the part of falling asleep. Reading a book assists us focusing, mental alertness, provide knowledge, rest to our senses and peace. It's damn underrated and what's the best part, anyone can do it anytime and anywhere without needed anybody else. It only needs a little curiosity and alertness. Steve Jobs said, take action when you feel scared. It gives you courage. In fear, we have two options, whether to go down or gearing up to build resilience, that's pure mindset.

Take a deep rest and then focus on your work deeply. By doing more work while exhausting ourselves, we destroy our focus & productivity too much. The great focus lies in taking more rest in between. *Some beautiful naps, a good book, a company of a true friend, a vacation, a slow sipping of tea, exploring nature, feeling physical intimacy, loving your people, staying stupid and laugh for long or just smiling at stupid moments.* Keep your habit of taking a rest before you get flushed out. You have to stop taking water out before the well gets empty.

One more reminder, when you are exhausted, accept it. Also, if you want to take a good rest, you have to utilise your high energy where you feel most satisfied. It's always a great rest when you accomplish the work you truly love. You can spend some time in luxury or wasting it as you want but first achieve your daily tasks and then you are good to go with your happiness but no regrets. ***Meanwhile, try sleeping as swift as possible and come out of bed as easy as you can.***

Merilyn Monroe is the most iconic Hollywood Sensual Star of all time and think about how she lived his leisure time. *When she had free time apart from filming movies & photoshoots, she spent her time simply in hotels or at home.* Yes, just this, that's it and she loved it.

Don't occupy yourself with too much of non-sense. Stay empty & idle, don't speak, just sit back and relax and you will find the purpose of your life. The major problem with our generation is they don't stop running to examine what they want and understand why they are running. You first need to know the right direction before starting a race because if you go far away, getting back from there would be extremely difficult.

The secret to change is to focus all of your energy not on

fighting the old, but on building the new. - Socrates.

Doing nothing is better than being busy doing nothing. - Lao Tzu.

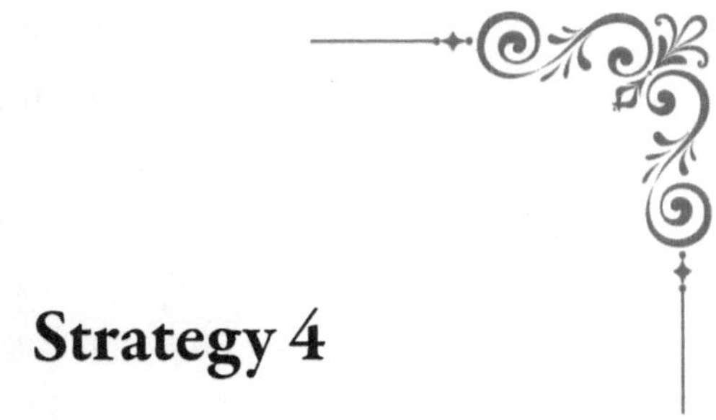

Strategy 4

Unveiling Your True Character & Soul - Bringing Out What You Want is Greater Than the World's Best: Know Yourself Honestly, Deeply and With Clarity

No one is hurt but by himself. - Diogenes.

Mahatma Gandhi once said, nobody can hurt me without my permission. Accepting truth about ourselves and doing the right act is the true courage of a soul. Diogenes, a cynic who once encountered Alexander the Great, criticizes the act of kindness & he would tease you if you helped an old lazy crossing the street. He would call it selfishness to fulfil your desire for kindness. *Diogenes once stated, if you ever want to think about yourself, you have to say the truth to yourself & speak the truth & that may harm the opinion of others.* What's the most difficult thing isn't the honesty towards others but our own soul because it's extremely difficult to face our wrongdoings. No one wants to feel guilty after analysing their own souls. So, they keep avoiding it until they meet the day by themselves. *We accept the truth when it remains the last option.*

Knowing our own character honestly, deeply and with clarity is the very first step towards knowing what we really seek. If you don't know what you want then every best thing would fascinate you a lot until you may find, it was never desired by you and not even fulfilling you. Smartly, you have to be very conscious and even oppose your own soul if you feel you are wrong.

If you want to know about yourself, first forget yourself, otherwise you will protect your soul with the wrongdoings. No one is hurting us but ourselves. The key to preventing being hurt is to accept the world as it is and try to work on yourself.

When *Nikola Tesla* was dying pennilessly in a hotel room at the age of 86, ***his last words were heart wrenching***. The man who invented Alternative Current Motors which is powering the entire world got broke. He said, ***'All these years that I had spent in the service of mankind brought me nothing but insults and humiliation.'*** His last words broke me too for long but he also believed, being abnormal is the only normal to remain excited for this life. We believe, whether it's happy or sad life but at least honest and that's what people realise at the end of their lives. When you are honest, you can be sad but can't be guilty for long. In that musing, you don't feel like you are hampering your everyday passion.

In some articles, I read, **Nikola Tesla** believed *a relationship with a woman consumes a lot of his focus and energy, so he chose science as his inspiration and shelter from a harsh life.* I feel, there was nothing wrong with it. A relationship requires a lot of love, involvement, dedication, and time. If you are passionate about something else, don't waste someone's time and life. That's the honest way to know yourself & others. We can't be perfect in everything, so we have to choose something that makes us feel passionate, honest and energetic.

Even **Charlie Chaplin** analysed his entire soul which was based on the **INFP** method which elaborates **Introverted, Intuitive, Feeling and Perceiving**. That's the most significant way of knowing your entire soul. If you can find out what you are, you are almost there in life. *Charlie Chaplin preferred solitude over socializing* because he wanted to pay more attention to his time in solitude to observe the world carefully. That's clever and brilliant. And here we are judging ourselves instead of knowing ourselves.

May be your weirdness & attributes are your uniqueness. What makes you different is what makes you unique. When you are born to stand out, why to stand in.

Another interesting fact I found out, people often seek their character's opinion from others. They try to find out their character on the judgement of others even though we all are entirely unique on our own scale. No one can even know how different we are and what we seek. So, if you want someone to push you for what you love, it's only you. You are the first worker at your work. You can see the magic in your work, not others. If you don't follow yourself, who else will. ***Don't ever reject yourself.***

Actors search for rejection. If they don't get it, they reject themselves. - Charlie Chaplin.

How much are you honest with your own soul? Do you even correct yourself when you feel you are wrong or you just try to cover by saying, it's okay! You know people are feeling difficult to choose what they love because they don't even know what they want and then they see what's the most desirable things in life and they all run towards them. Is it possible that everyone had the same goals? When we were children, we chose what we really loved. An honest man is always a child. And now when we are growing up, we are becoming partial to ourselves. See what you loved as a child and you will love it forever even with consciousness; forever, no matter what. Intelligence is stupid sometimes.

Can you feel, the fear of failure can make you the best in the world? Steve Jobs literally had a fear of failure which made him perfectionist & helped him pushing himself ahead & others to do great things. Along with it, most people don't know Steve Jobs locked himself away for 3 days before each of the Apple conferences. No one knows, he had to work extremely hard at public speaking.

Now, what's the most significant attribute a person should have instead of deliberately finding it in his own soul and if he doesn't have that, he should practice it; a great sense of humour. *A great sense of humour is extremely appealing in a character and allure other people towards your charisma.* It's evident that Nikola Tesla had a great sense of humour and even the world's best people have a great sense of humor that keeps them attractive for long. It's definitely true, a happy character is always more beautiful, charming and attractive and he can do arduous work very easily like a child playing effortlessly. In gist, Steve Jobs taught me, when no one understands your vision, take chances of your own passion & the masses will follow.

You know, you are special. I'm special. We all are special & that's the power of us. We all are our characters and our differences are our own powers.

If you want to be yourself and know yourself deeply in the right way, Stoicism can help you out in the best way. **Stoicism** teaches us to focus on the things we can control; our thoughts, emotions and actions while accepting the things we don't. *A Stoic is being calm and almost without any emotion.* While knowing your character in deep, the best key to a good life is self-control, discipline, acceptance and stopping trying to control everything. A Stoic love people deeply and unashamedly.

Seneca explained, 'He is the most powerful who has power over himself.' Also, a great conscious human can be predicted by when he finds something very true by his own consciousness instead of accepting or knowing it. The true consciousness already exists everywhere.

Being silly is very underrated. It's just one life and we are forced to be artificial. **Ludwig Wittgenstein said, 'If people never did silly things, nothing intelligent would ever get done.'** You know, we aren't even honest with ourselves because we are afraid of our own souls because mostly, we all are wrong. Diogenes taught us the life of shamelessness where he tried to find himself instead of following the masses. His purpose in life was to secure a happy life. He depicted, *"I know not* *how to conceive the good, apart from pleasure of taste, sexual pleasures, the pleasures of sound and the pleasures of beautiful form."* He rejected the concept of "manners" as a lie and focuses on complete truth fullness at all times and under any circumstances. He preferred honest living with complete freedom of speech.

The art of being a slave is to rule one's master. - Diogenes of Sinope - Masterpiece and Brilliant at the same time.

Plato famously sounded, Knowledge without justice ought to be called cunning rather than wisdom. The first & greatest victory is to conquer yourself; to be conquered by yourself is of all things most shameful & vile.

You know, we are afraid of ourselves because we are wrong. We don't accept the wrong in our own souls. We don't want to change because we don't want to destroy our illusions. What's our true character! You should know yourself without judgement to find out what's your obsession then you should seek to make it right. Adolf Hitler, once said, if you tell a big enough lie and tell it frequently enough it will be believed. Now think, are you sure, you aren't telling lies to yourself!

We have found some most significant highlights to make and

assist you to scrounge & remember your true character:

- Until you find yourself with your most loving obsession, you will find every illusion & thing as an absolute truth to make your soul happy. *We don't become happy with what we get but what we really want and get the same.*

- There's a **Japanese Pastel Nagomi Art** that impose no restrictions or rules of 'correctness' ultimately which allows Japanese to freely reflect their own identity. It's not focused on right or wrong but they *try to develop a sense of harmony in diversity.*

- ***If you want to know yourself, write for yourself.*** Are you keeping a diary of your experiences like **Anne Frank** did?

- After knowing himself, **Franz Kafka** realised he was more creative at night and that makes us astonish, a genius can come in any form.

- ***Plato voiced, Man is a being in search of a meaning and if the purpose is evil then knowledge becomes evil. He also famously said, before they can read you & implement you, they would know what you do with them. Most people ultimately follow your character. That's damn true.***

- Start with the man in the mirror. Start with yourself. Don't be looking at the all other things. Start with your own soul.

- *If you aren't listening to yourself, no one will.*

- If you want to be right and true to yourself, don't do wrongdoings to others even if they try to bring you down. They would get destroyed with their own consciousness. *Socrates said, 'One should never do wrong in return, nor mistreat any man, no matter how one has been mistreated by him.'* He often said, 'The greatest way to live with honour in this world is to be what we pretend to be.'

- Before you fly, develop strong wings. Wings are the place to fly for happiness at any time you want.

- You can purely know yourself when you protect your time and give sufficient time to yourself to calm down. Because when you have time for yourself then you can bring out what you have stuffed inside for years. It's strange we sense a lot of things & incidents, events, experiences, love, hate, friendship and more but have nothing to say. When you stay alone with yourself you can find your character to find your life obsession. Don't ever question, just exist with yourself truly & you will find the answers. Be honest with yourself.

- ***You are unique in something. We all are unique in something.*** Maybe we want to succeed in what we love but sometimes we are forced to choose the most successful path. The truth, the key to a great life is to choose what you love and you will be successful. If you have a unique key, don't try to unlock the small or big doors but exactly the same lock that belongs to you.

- ***To know your own character, we have to be extremely conscious of what we do.*** With every right & wrong we do, we already become conscious but ignore the impact & effects of wrong deeds in our own ego, pleasure and wants.

- *Sometimes judge yourself to know why you aren't doing your best.* Say yourself, you deserve what you truly love and that's best.

- ***Think for yourself honestly.*** Before you are anyone else, you are the world's best person ever existed, now do the same, you are already.

- Even if the entire world tells you that you are right & if you still feel you are wrong, you are wrong my buddy. We can't betray ourselves. We should be extremely honest with ourselves. It's just we hide & protect our own energy from our truth. ***Grow up and heal.***

- Use your high IQ & potential in the right direction & it will get recognised when you become an artist, writer or painter or equivalent to create some art then it will be seen otherwise your high potential & overthinking is a threat & they can make your life hell. *Use your potential in the right direction.*

- ***Confucius stated, a great man is hard on himself; a small man is hard on others.*** Also, he remarked, What the superior man seeks is in himself; what the small man seeks in others.

- I felt, it's not the type of relationship with people that develops our behaviour but our character. People choose characters first even before buying small value products.

- You can't be yourself unless you become dead for the entire universe. ***Ralph Waldo Emerson proclaimed, Self-trust is the first secret to success.*** Further he added, to be yourself in a world that is constantly trying to make you something else is the greatest accomplishment.

- When you are wrong in your character, you will oppose what is right because it would go against your illusion. Be right in your character & the act of doing right will become very easy for you.

- Marcus Aurelius said a great quote, we love ourselves more than other people, but care about their opinions more than our own.

All humans are mere actors to become what the world seeks from them. The only time they are honest is when they are angry.

The final forming of a person's character lies in their own hands. - Anne Frank.

I wish they would take me as I am. - Vincent Van Gogh.

The Art of Never Giving Up: How to Develop the Never Give Up Attitude

Purpose of the Strategy: *Mastering the Art of Perseverance for Limitless Success & Fulfilment & Perceiving the True Power to Go Far in Life and Chase Obsession.*

You make your own luck if you stay at it long enough - Naval Ravikant.

Who a great painter is! The man who paints his own dreams irrespective of thinking about whether the people would like him or not! Who a great Writer is! The man who writes about absolute truth, beauty and love even when he fails and doesn't care about whether the people would love him or not. To become honest about your obsession, first you have to make your soul free from every opinion, fear, love, hate or any rejection. ***Bob Newhart said, 'The greatest comedian I've ever seen is Jack Benny. He wasn't afraid of silences.'*** And this is marvellous. An awkward silence can break the confidence of any comedian. ***Obsession isn't for people but for our own souls.***

If you are working to please people, you would discourage and disappoint yourself because in expecting what you want you can't fulfil your soul with what you want. *The first thing that can make you unbeatable is your honesty to yourself.* When you know what you want, you become crystal clear. People feel success as a different concept and it usually perceives as extremely hard. Of course, it's arduous but if you aren't following yourself, you can't even accomplish the easiest but if you are doing what you love the most, you can even accomplish the hardest. ***A true success is itself free from any success or failure but get fulfilled with your own satisfaction, that's it.*** That will take you in the long run. People run towards success because that's the only proof they would have to show in identification that they are successful but in reality, when you choose the work you truly love from the heart and can go to any length to make it happen, that's pure obsession. That makes you unbeatable. You would never ever give up with that.

In reality, you can also beat the man with hard work who doesn't love his work because if you are giving pain to your soul, the pain would rise and at the end you would leave everything. Money, success, wealth, people, & fame all aren't the keys to success. It's your self-obsession towards your deep work.

According to research conducted by the ***National Science Foundation around 80% of our thoughts are negative & we have around 60,000 thoughts on an average day.*** Can you imagine this? Human civilisation always had the same problem of being negative because we are designed like this. Most people give up on their work because they usually start their work with some motivation or desire. As their motivation shakes or desires get fulfilled, they become slow or halt their journey. A true obsessed person is free from such desires or the fear of failure. ***In 2015, when I started my writing career during my graduation days, I was literally upset even after scoring well.*** There was some tumult in my soul and every day I was feeling like something was missing. I was a complete bookworm, an introvert and a man whose legs trembled as soon as the lecturer called his name. I also wanted to be a lecturer but fortunately, I found my passion and followed it well. Trust me, I'm naive in writing. I just try to make it simple and write the absolute truth. Nothing extraordinary. In the beginning of a few years of my writing career, I got miserably failed financially but I was never attached to any of the factors. I was extremely glad & satisfied doing it, that's it. I was getting peaceful sleep and became energetic day by day. I also found where we all lose the control of our satisfaction. If you are keeping it outside, you have to beg for it from the external factors again and again. You can't be happy in success and sad in failure, that would not work. So, anytime I was doing research on my book and writing it, I was creating energy and literally I wasn't getting consumed. We all have such work where we don't get consumed but become energetic and that's our internal locus of control. Even after 8 years, my skills have been enhancing and I have become obsessed with it. My books still fail financially but that wasn't the motive for which I began it. I never started for money, wealth or fame. I just find myself truly and that makes me feel worthy & unbeatable.

Aristotle explained, 'You will never do anything in this world without courage. It's the greatest quality of the mind next to honour.' Even Alexander the Great depicted, each moment free from fear makes a man immortal and there's nothing impossible to him who will try. I'm also impressed when he said, **with the right attitude, self-imposed limitations vanish.** It's damn true, no one is stopping us. Fear, failure, success, wealth, money, opinions, & rejections all come from outside to inside but a true obsessed person lives from inside to outside. That's the best way to laugh even when the entire world crashes & become gloomy.

Martin Luther King suggested to us the best lessons to never lose hope, open up against the things that are wrong and trust the process. He said, if you can't fly, then run. If you can't run, then walk. If you can't walk, then crawl. But whatever you do, you have to keep moving forward. He suggested us to stick to love for easy living, forgiving people easily, and face the challenges to build strength. **We feel, don't try to live risk free, that's the biggest risk of life.**

What's your true excuse? When *Stephen Hawking was 21, he was diagnosed with motor neurone disease (MND). It affects the brain cells that communicate with the body muscles.* And later in curiosity he said, **'If you understand how the universe operates, you control it in a way. However difficult life may see there is always something you can do and succeed at. Good luck to you all. It matters that you don't just give up.'**

Marie Curie who was the master of simplification, did most of her research in an old shed behind her husband's Pierre school. If it's truly significant to you, you will surely find a way instead of giving up because the pain of regret is harder than the pain of working hard. She remarked, *'Now is the time to understand more so that we may fear less. You must never be fearful of what you are doing when it is right.'*

Most people aren't aware, *Franz Kafka* wasn't widely published when he was alive. ***He faced a lot of rejection.*** Even when he was living his last days, he instructed his friend Brod to burn all of his manuscripts, including his letters and diaries but he still published all of them and now because of Brod Contribution, Nikola Tesla is the most popular writer of all time. ***The fear of your own judgement can kill your best work. Right Confidence plays a significant role on making what you love.***

A Few More Tips to Build the Great Resilience to Never Ever Giving Up Attitude:

- *We all will grow into the work we love & everyday else will fall off somehow.* The intense force to do great work is to first find out what you love & you don't have to chase anything after that in your life.

- *Bound yourself to targets when you are the owner of your routine.* Bound yourself to extreme targets, the impossible ones. Build impossible skills, that's how you would fly.

- *Be super conscious of what you are choosing in life as your primary work.* Even if the entire world crashes, I will make you super conscious of your power so that even if you get fail you would also rise from the ashes.

- *Only passionate people can conclude the world's impossible work because they really want to.*

- Also, the life of Diogenes is the best instance to live a great life even when you have nothing. It's not attached to failure or success but honesty to your own soul. Even when he was homeless, penniless & even got enslaved at some point in his life, he remained honest with his life. That honesty makes you unbeatable in life.

- It's not about success or failure of life that decides the course of happiness & peace but how well we were in those times, that's the process of great living, that's the real life we taste ourselves with our attitude.

- I have deeply learned, most philosophers, people around the world, books & everything deliver the same message; to know ourselves & have some courage to do the impossible because at the end, you would find you may get more courage than before but not the time. Fear is stupid. I have seen people who were afraid the entire life like what worst would happen to them. It's not the worst that would impact you but your mindset. People often blame failure but fear is not the actual reason because we only wanted to get succeed because that's the only factor to make us feel satisfied. Bullshit. Time is the wealth that can't be returned in any case.

- Conquer yourself, free yourself from fear, scream, cry but learn the deep courage, madness and no one can stop you from what you seek.

- ***Don't ever fear from immense darkness.*** A ray of light is enough to kill darkness. Stick to what you love & you will definitely find yourself. Bill Gates said, to win big, you sometimes have to take big risks.

- Remember, when you think about giving up, maybe you are at the phase of going high into the sky to touch heaven.

- Focus more on improvement than failure. ***Bill Gates said, embrace bad news to learn where you need the most*** *improvement.* Even Jeff Bezos depicted the same thing, *if you can't tolerate critics, don't do anything new or interesting.*

And when your heart is heavy & every second thing you do feel wasted & your eyes remain on your goal, obsession, soul & eyes can't resist & even if you have failed many times before & still you are running towards it, then what would you do? And you are feeling more love and falling in love with your work even more; when giving up isn't bothering you. When nights become brightest. Loneliness doesn't bother you & you can still work even when you are exhausted. My friend, then you have found what you truly love. It's the only love that will make you genius and it will matter to you in any conditions & you will perceive everything else as a pure distraction and still feel extremely sure in what you are doing. Trust me, your soul is on the right track, my friend. **You know, distraction has pleasure but no peace. Love is still the greatest power in the world.**

If you hear a voice within you say, you cannot paint, then by all means paint, and that voice will be silenced. - Vincent Van Gogh.

These are the most powerful words said by Vincent Van Gogh when he was an utter failure in front of people. He clarified sadly, 'If I am worth anything later, I am worth something now. For wheat is wheat in the beginning, even if people think it is grass in the beginning.'

Marilyn Monroe was a powerful & determined iconic woman who never stopped trying to make her life more fulfilling against the odds. She even survived *sexual child abuse* and more obstacles in her time. As the most popular classic actress of all time, she fought for her dreams and then after she famously said, *'Fear is stupid. So are regrets.'*

Strategy 6

The True Power of Purposeful Work for Creating Limitless Energy & Achievement - Rising Work Energy vs Wrong Work Energy

Purpose of the Strategy: How to create energy through your work instead of consuming yourself with the work - How to stop time for the work - How to get more energetic – Comfort zone is the real truth - How to dance forever in life – How to keep creating & working on what you love.

We are asleep. Our life is a dream, but we wake up sometimes, just enough to know that we are dreaming. - Ludwig Wittgenstein.

The world is divided between two kinds of personalities, consumed and energetic. If you observe around yourself, you will find a lot of people doing arduous work for their livelihood. They all feel like they are doing hard work and that's what our parents teach us; do the hard work. We all feel work as a burden and we have to do it even when we don't like it. Once there was *Vincent Van Gogh who was crafting paintings one after other even though he never got recognition in his entire life but now his paintings are fetching billions* and ***Nikola Tesla who died penniless in a cheap hotel all alone but gave human existence an alternative current motor that is lighting the entire world.*** So, even after failures, they were still highly energetic to do what they wanted. What's their real secret of being energetic? First, Understand, energy can be faked in the short run. Truly, energy can be faked for so long until our mind gets burst out and we may feel extremely dissatisfied within our souls. I found some people are extremely lethargic even with the best things because they aren't placed where they should or wanted to be. There are multiple sources for energies for a soul but as soon as the sources get diminished with the passing of life i.e. time, we realise the power of energies we were getting from the external sources. It means, dependency. We have to depend on someone or something else to remain energetic, so the fluctuations can make us gloomy too so, how better I would be if we keep the power within ourselves!

Our internet generation is really doing extremely hard because that's what we were taught. ***Do hard work to achieve the things we want but there's a misconception. You can't do hard work for long in the process you don't love.*** Most desires are based on best results. Those who do hard work get consumed very easily during the process and don't even realise the best of their lives. If you are feeling every second of your work, you are not completely focused or obsessed. You can't go for too long to do your best work but the best would happen, when you get lost into the work completely. You slow down your energy consumption and sometimes you won't even realise that you are working hard. It's not only a play but it's more than that, like you are focusing on something you love and you will not get more exhausted even after doing work for so long and even you would feel much energetic after the process. That's the true power of creating energy in the process of work you love.

Hard work is for those who are pressuring themselves with something they don't want. ***You don't ever have to pressurize otherwise it wouldn't go for too long.*** Whether we talk about Merilyn Monroe, Nikola Tesla, Pablo Picasso, Franz Kafka or Vincent Van Gogh, they were extremely obsessed with the process of their work. They felt extremely satisfied even before the results of their own work and that makes them energetic after that. And trust me, when your soul is satisfied with your work, you are already winning and making yourself truly. You don't need any medal from anyone to prove your success.

Once *Alexander the Great* elaborated, *'Without knowledge, skill cannot be focused. Without skill, strength cannot be brought to bear and without strength, knowledge may not be applied.'* We feel, the culture of hard work is wrongly presented to our generation. If someone just chooses what he truly loves for himself, and works on it honestly, then it's purely a play but what we can do because we are also fascinated by status, money, wealth and power and that makes up choosing the best and we even feel good until these factors get vanished with time. The only factor that would remain with us is our curiosity and love. Love increases with time. It doesn't get diminished at any step.

You know, the famous sports shoe company ***Adidas was started in a washroom*** where the first electricity room was prepared to make the shoes and then they conquered the world. We went through their website where they mentioned, *'We've done our best for the best. We've improved & grown. Looking ahead to the future, always remembering where we came from. This is our story.'*

Adidas literally seized the opportunities and has become the best in the market.

- ***How to Dance Forever in Your Life:*** The work! Your work should fascinate you a lot before anyone else. You may feel like dancing after doing it immediately. If it's missing then for what we are doing our work. People get tired of the work they don't love or forcing themselves to work on something else. When you love something, you don't need motivation but just solitude & you will dance again, once again, ever and forever.

- ***Keep Creating & Working:*** You know, the most intense arts are primarily enjoyed by the artists first. The details are the instances of how deep someone can go into something to make it finest ever.

- ***How to Get More Time & Energy:*** Always try creating more time & energy to do the work you love because after doing what you love, you may get physically exhausted but still mentally energetic and happy. Don't ever consume yourself by doing the work you don't cherish.

- We can't skip the pain but we can still smile during those times, at least!

- We feel, ***comfort zone is the real truth.*** Take extreme pain & obsession for the work you love and you will still feel easy and don't take pain while doing the work you don't love. When you create something, you are energetic but when you miss the love and creation, you are consumed.

- Always try getting happy with the little work you have done but don't stop with the happiness of the little work accomplishment. Go forward even in success. Don't stop.

- Ludwig Wittgenstein had a logic behind his philosophy & he depicted, 'The world is what we make of it.'

- Its damn significant to perceive, intelligent people don't make history. Only the obsessed, smart, skilled and ordinary people with discipline make history but we see them as extraordinary because they follow themselves. You don't have to be extraordinary but ordinary with working on yourself & skills and you can even beat the genius easily.

- To follow your fire, build your charisma, aura, vibe, a soul and a true energy to yourself to make your dream come true. *Martin Luther King Jr. was really a charm attic man & really energetic.*

- *Energies don't lie.* If you want to learn about your enemy, see how much energy he's injecting to hate you; how much energy he's serving to love himself. See, your enemy would get fail because he will burn himself in that negative fire & you will grow yourself in a good fire. Good fire is truly good colours to our artistic hearts.

- Researches say some simple facts on productivity like *nothing good happens after 2AM*, it's very difficult to get great productivity after 3PM, There's decline in productivity after 4PM and we should take proper breaks, naps and rests to recharge our potential.

- *You know, everything is non sense if you aren't interested and curious. Be curious and interested.*

- Some people are themselves are art. They should be praised differently from every angle.

- To become highly successful in your work, first forget it's the damn hard work. Take it easy; Take it lightly & that's how you can do the best work of your life.

- Don't put the high energy into the work where you can be less energetic but it's not allowed to be less energetic in the work you love because that would hamper your real potential and true productivity.

What's Your True Comfort Zone: Always try to understand your god gifted soulful work, a work that make you feel like dancing; that make you feel the music of your own heart; the work that would make your heart pounding on your chest; the work you would still choose even in the most stressful situations; that you will still choose for your last day, that's your obsession & that's the work you will follow for life. To give life a great meaning, you should worship what you really love from your heart, otherwise you will do only a hard labour throughout your life. I feel this is much significant. It's just one life, my friend, learn, your true comfort zone is where your true energy resides.

We should seek the greatest value of our actions. - Stephen Hawking.

Intelligence without Ambition is a bird without wings. - Salvador Dali.

Strategy 7

The Energy of Loving Work > The Energy of the Best in the World – Acquiring Deep Peace

> Exaggerate the essential and leave the obvious vague. - Vincent Van Gogh.

Do you know yourself honestly? *Socrates intellectualism depicts, a new one will do what is right or best just soon as one truly understands about them.* Our world pulls us towards the best but we should seek what we truly love from our heart. The work we would choose even while taking our last breaths. We have analysed more than 100 influential personalities irrespective of their success or failure rate but obsession with their work. How people can be so obsessed with something that people call them mad. *If you have ever found a painter who is painting 14 hours a day, then would you call him a mad person.* Of course, we think of these personalities as mad people, highly obsessed people. When people say, I want the best, I laugh my ass off because I know soon, they will be tired as soon as they get it. There's no destination in obsessed work but only a journey to be enjoyed intensely.

What a beautiful day, I articulate Pablo Picasso last day really an enchanting and soulful day. *An article in Time Magazine in 1973 clarified; on his final day, Pablo Picasso had dinner with his friends and after he entered the studio and painted till 3am. The next morning, he was no more. He took his last breath and got dead with his soulful experience. What's the use of the best if you can't make your soul satisfied!* People usually think they have enough time to feel satisfied but till then they get already consumed with the best of this world. Every creature in this universe has their own capabilities and powers and these capabilities are far better than seeking the best. ***Michael Jackson said, If I'm not creating, I'm not as happy.*** Even the world's best dancer wasn't happy when he was not dancing. We all are forcing interest in ourselves in the hope of getting satisfied but that's go until we realise that's not what I wanted. When you love something that makes your soul satisfied, you go beyond success or failure. You will do it in any situation of life whether you have everything or nothing, that's the true power of loving work. You will reach the level of impossibility and win the entire universe flawlessly. Best is worst if you aren't interested. We have been growing in such an environment where we are usually given limited options to choose instead of finding and understanding our own character and passion and doing what we really want. So, whatever we choose, we force ourselves and everything feels tough. That's simple and deep too. ***Why do I have to fly when I want to***

walk? There's a race to become the best but you can be the world's best flawlessly when you choose what you love. *Naval Ravikant said, the smarter you get, the slower you read.* Because that makes you realise the true value of silence between the words. We feel every work is a work of art. You can be creative and energetic in anything you want even if you do a routine job. The level of your entertainment depends on you, and for that, you don't need the best but what you immensely seek. When you really want to run, you will run beyond race, that's the true power of obsession. The power of loving work is far greater than the power of the best. The best will stop you as soon as you get it but a true love will go on even if you get it more than required.

Some Heart-Warming Tips for More Self-Love:

- We mentioned earlier, being abnormal is the only normal to remain excited for this life.

- At the end of life, **what matter is how we feel & everything else is just a waste of time.** A true feeling is definitely significant to feel great in life.

- **Steve Jobs**, the founder of Apple Inc. said, **the only way to do great work is to love what you do. If you haven't found it yet, keep looking, don't settle.**

- Most people choose the most loving work as a side work of their life but they should keep it as the vital part.

- You know, **the last words of Kurt Cobain thrilled me. He said, 'It's better to burn out than fade away.'** We feel, life is all about making it intense for everyday life. This day will never ever come back. Can we even realise this? It's your choice whether you want to go for what you love and it's okay even if it's not the best.

- You have to run the race when you are in the competition. Most people forget they can choose their own loving track or make it on the way.

- I have learned, the biggest failure is when you succeed in an uninterested work and the biggest success is when you succeed in the work you truly love & even if it doesn't matter to anybody else.

- To give something more than 100%, the impossibility, you have to love the work intensely or choose the things you truly love because where you can be mad and with madness, there's no existence of impossibility.

- Take the first step in what you love the most and soon you will see the entire way as you walk ahead.

- You know, **Japanese people** have a great sense of process to live life with great intensity that makes them stress free, peaceful and happy. *They often get criticized for their simple living and overall, they are happy and prosperous and that's what matter.*

- Remember this, don't ever win on someone else's expectations. Win on your own rules. If you aren't satisfied with the world's best, throw it out. You know yourself. Complete yourself and then seek others. ***Do what's best for you instead of seeking the best.***

- Set big loving goals that excites you & every set of goals should be your most loved interest even if you are an amateur in that interest. As it's your most loved interest, you will definitely improve in any conditions because it's truly significant for your soul satisfaction & one day you will develop the potential & become the person you truly love.

- If you are writing a book, think, *well designed books rarely get read but a good book can be read anytime.* Come out of the product life cycle and create something for eternity.

- Don't ever worry about the result when you are doing the hard work. Also, I read somewhere, don't create & analyse at the same time. You may hamper your best work while seeking and expecting results.

- Various articles suggested, *Marie Curie was an inexhaustible energy with a deep work obsession.* She was insanely interested in what she was doing. She literally described as a maniacal worker or a mad scientist. Analysing her personality, we think we don't need our best but we need what we love, that sparks our soul and that's enough for this life.

- Choose the right most loving work and you will forget about success or failure but it's the sense of satisfaction that's what the human soul needs. *When we choose what we don't love, we try to fulfil our soul from other sources and as these sources fluctuate, our satisfaction fluctuates because we are seeking it from outside.*

- ***Pablo Picasso*** had the habit of finding out the strength and weakness of art including his own. He made his artistic life his daily job. *He painted every day until his last day even at the age of 91. That's pure soul satisfaction and irresistible obsession.*

- *William Shakespeare is the perfect instance of being an irresistible obsessed with doing your loving work.* He was incredibly productive as he wrote 37 plays, 154 sonnets & a few poems. You can't believe it, he wrote the world's best plays like *Hamlet, Romeo and Juliet or Julias Ceaser with an average of 1.5 plays a year.* That's an incredible instance of the possibility of the impossibility of your loving work.

- ***Merilyn Monroe depicted, it's better to be hated for what you are than to be loved for what you're not.***

- If you are forcing something on your soul, heart and mind, you can't be creative and even if you can't stay all alone with yourself, then who else will?

- If you live for yourself, devote yourself to the most loving art & get lost into it. You may miss the outside world but, not yourself. You have to find yourself, that's the point of having this life.

- ***Discipline is easy when you are going with the flow of your own soul.***

- It's amazing to get a little successful in the work you love than highly successful in the work you don't even love.

Choose a job you love and you will never have to work a day in your life. - Confucius.

Strategy 8

The Real Strength of an Artist - Every work is an Art - Stay Hyper Alert

Purpose of the Strategy: What's the power of a true loving work? - How to create the world's best MASTERPIECE flawlessly.

The earth has music for those who listen. - William Shakespeare.

How to win the hearts of the audience? How to create the Masterpiece that makes you eternal for life? Pablo Picasso consoled, If I paint a wild horse, you might not see the horse but surely you will see the wildness! Every work in this universe is a work of art but most people see their work as an ordinary task. We believe, artists have better learnings of life while concluding what they love instead of pushing themselves to something they don't love.

Artists live better in reality & retrospection. They love themselves too much & try finding the interest of their souls and create truth with high intensity. If you think this chapter isn't for you, just because you aren't an artist, then you should take more interest in that now. That's the first rule of being an artist, be curious about things he perceives. History says artists live even after death & History is often remembered by them and above all, it's a great myth that we aren't artists. Everyone is an artist. It's not only the painters, writers, dancers, directors or musicians who are artists but everyone. If you aren't using your artistic capabilities in your work, you are pushing yourself slowly to get consumed. *A normal person may get consumed with his work but an artist creates intense energy in his work.* If you feel like you aren't doing what you love then start loving what you have right now. Even a man who is working in a genius call centre can bring up his great energy by taking a deep interest in his work. It's a pure journey from a normal person to an artistic person who enjoys every moment of his work. We realised, most people are doing work just for the sake of money than taking a real interest in their work. It's also true, even anyone can be a writer and wouldn't be a great artist until he follows the rules of an artist.

Neil Gaiman says, 'When things get tough, this is what you should do. Make good art.' An artist lives better than anyone else in this world and he creates a few powers that make him incredibly obsessed and special. We have found a few that make you feel like dancing while carrying out your work. The first attribute is high intensity. *We feel the outcome of your work is directly related to how much you are interested in that.* If you are curious, interested and energetic, your outcome will be extremely good. Also, your outcome depends on how energetic you are while carrying out and at what level of emotional stability. Your emotions are your power. Whether he was Vincent Van Gogh, Pablo Picasso, Franz Kafka, Nikola Tesla or Marie Curie; these personalities injected intense emotions into their work. They weren't true genius but truly interested in what they were doing and at last, they automatically got up ended with the world's best work because they were purely interested. Their love, aura, vibes, heart, truth, soul, nature and beauty were with their true art attributes and finally, they ended up with the *Masterpieces*.

Diogenes explained, 'Of what use is a philosopher who doesn't hurt anybody's feelings.' Artists often try to live life while learning it. They try to find the absolute truth through sadness and energy. In our books, we mentioned Nature is an absolute truth because it gives the same pleasure every time, we expect from it. God is a great philosopher who created this world as an art and to understand its every atom, we have to be an intense artist.

After researching, analysing history and learning about world's best personalities, we have concluded a few things that would help you to become the great artists of your work. It doesn't matter whether you are or not but by learning you can be highly energetic after implementing these tips:

- If you want to be a great artist, develop a great photogenic memory where you can still remember the exact details of the events as you live them. It helps you remember moments, happiness and love. ***Nikola Tesla had the great photogenic memory for remembering events well. He was known to memorize books & had a powerful imagination.***

- Sometimes our art makes us sad and that's why most people avoid being creative and hyper active with their consciousness because it hampers their lies and make them gloomy with the truth of life. ***Naval Ravikant depicted, 'Art is anything done for its own sake.'*** We feel, art can make you sad but even after you will enjoy it very well.

- ***Your charm & energy is your art.*** Share your creativity with others, your friends, your partner & others because for an artist, doing what he loves is an energetic fuel & also, if you are allowed to do it naturally, you may feel your charm & at last your way of style of accomplishing things.

- *Every life is itself an art.* We all paint with our own brushes. Some have dark bright colours, some have faded while some have black & white but we all have some colours and that's what's significant for an artist. Every moment spent living for yourself isn't wasted. Be kind to yourself before others. Be creative, enthusiastic, intelligent, energetic, have great sense of humor, stay witty and passionate.

- Following your soul is very easy. ***According to cynicism, living according to nature & not human related customs is the highest form of wisdom.*** We should follow our energy then satisfy the entire world. Don't oppose your soul and nature if you want to achieve great wisdom & success in life.

- ***Aristotle said, 'No great mind has ever existed without a touch of madness.'*** If you want to stand out, stay mad. Normal is very normal these days. Every best will get ignored if it's normal.

Study suggests a few rules to win the hearts of audience

- *Always deliver your message with great energy and intensity.*

- *Always lead by a true example.*

- *Have great anecdotes - Great Tales.*

- Think about others than yourself.

- Use Japanese Concept IKIGAI.

- Win audience hearts than their minds.

- Have meaningful missions like Martin Luther King Jr.

- Many people aren't aware of the fact, ***Adolf Hitler once had an artistic dream. When he was young, he had a dream of becoming a painter.*** In 1907, he applied to Vienna Academy of Art but failed twice in taking admission there. Even when his mother died of breast cancer, he lived his next four years on the streets of Vienna. During that time, he tried to sell his postcards of his artworks while staying in homeless shelters. He even worked as a casual labourer & sold paintings of Vienna's various sites too. It's damn true, an artist is usually going from inside to outside & paints himself the tragedy of this world. ***In 2002, a modern art critic reviewed Adolf Hitler's paintings and found the style in which he painted the human figures showed that he had a little interest in people. Adolf Hitler was never much interested in the emotions of people.***

- The writer of ***Norwegian Woods***, ***Haruki Murakami*** clarified, ***'With my eyes closed, I would touch a familiar book & draw its fragrance deep inside me. This was enough to make me happy.'***

- I have learned from all the creators, master of arts, students, teachers, philosophers, artists and God that simplicity matters. ***It's not the difficult things that touch Zenith but the simple and emotional ones.*** Capture your audience, win their hearts & you can win the entire world.

- I read an article on the internet and found, ***Haruki Murakami*** writing process is very bizarre. As most writers try making the ending & decide it well before the writing process but when he writes, he doesn't know about its overall conclusion. *Instead, he loves to find out the endings on his way while going deep into the writing process.*

- We feel an artist shouldn't have deadlines. **Even Murakami doesn't like deadlines.** In a 2014 interview to the Guardian, he elaborated, 'When it's finished, it's finished, but before then it is not finished.' Great literature & arts don't require deadlines. Let it open and once it's done, you will already know it otherwise you will rush to finish it somehow but it should be accomplished intensely.

- Instead of spending huge money on advertisements, better you try knowing what your customers want because a good customer can find out what he really desires. You don't have to run behind them all the time.

- Your greatest work for humanity is truth & honesty, whether it's good or bad, happy or sad, just be honest & true to yourself.

- Never ever think you aren't an artist. Every work is a work of art even when you are doing a clerical job. We don't disgrace any job you have. If you can find anything interesting & bring up something good in your work, you can do anything.

- *Franz Kafka stated, 'Writing is a sweet, wonderful reward.' And as a writer, I can feel it. After that he said some heart throbbing words too, 'A non-writing writer is a monster counting insanity.'* Therefore, once you find out the motive of your life you have to keep doing what you love, at least for your soul.

- An artist never misses the details, never ever. It's how these details actually make him a true artist. That's the true process. That's how the spectators get astounded; that's how an artist feels satisfied when he finds out everything in between, & that's what a true love of an artist is.

- *An artist is purely obsessed.* Vincent Van Gogh was extremely busy during his time. As an artist, he created 2100 artworks including 860 oil paintings but at last he said his last words, *'The sadness will last forever.'*

- The great philosopher, *Aristotle invented rhetoric, the true art of persuasion.* His general advice to public speakers and writers was to recognize your audience's emotions, so you can establish a connection with them. We feel, we should always leave our audience astonished & with a question & that's how they will find the right answers with their consciousness.

- The world-famous director of Classic Movies, *Alfred Hitchcock* clarified, *'The length of the film should be directed related to the endurance of the human bladder.'* Also, he expressed, 'If it's a good movie, the sound could go off and the audience would still have a perfectly clear idea of what was going on.' Also, he added, *'Art is a technique of communication. The image is the most complete technique of all communication. I always take the audience into account.'*

- If you want to be a great artist, choose reality no matter how dark it is. People would really love it. They all want truths, harsh truths, their own truths that aren't usually appreciated in society. Plato once said, 'No one is more hated than he who speaks the truth.'

- Art should be deep, delicious and filled with emotions and arouse your curiosity. *Pablo Picasso paintings are priceless because of the depth of creativity. His art is deep & true.*

- There's a pure research on the inspiration paradox that depicts your best creative time is not when you think. We feel your best creative time is when you are not thinking about it but something else. The time in which you are absolutely normal with yourself.

- A big myth; most artists try to create what can sell easily and that can exhaust themselves in the long run. Pablo Picasso revealed, *'An artist is a person who paints what you can sell. A good artist is a person who sells what he paints.'* It's like you are selling yourself in the form of art, not the art people seek. Artists work isn't to please the audience but to serve them with reality. Also, if you want to stay fresh, increase your artistic capabilities & stand out. Don't copy or repeat yourself. *For that Picasso said, 'To copy others is necessary, but to copy oneself is pathetic.'*

- Art can be an illusion. Picasso mentioned, *'Why do you try to understand art? Do you try to understand the song of a bird?'* He also said, 'Good taste is the enemy of creativity.'

- As an artist your life is an inspiration to other people. *Salvador Dali* observed, 'A true artist is not one who is inspired but one who inspires others. He also clarified beautifully, *'The first man to compare the cheeks of a young woman to a rose was obviously a poet; the first one to repeat it was possibly an idiot.'*

- As an artist, I feel, Imitation isn't wrong but imitation is also an art. Salvador Dali depicted, those who do not want to imitate anything, produce nothing.'

- This is damn significant for an artist, an extreme solitude. *There's nothing pleasurable than idleness & silence for an artist.*

It is very important for young people to keep their sense of wonder and keep asking why. - Stephen Hawking.

I paint what I think, not what I see. - Pablo Picasso.

Art is to console those who are broken by life. - Vincent Van Gogh.

Strategy 9

The Supremacy of Accepting Adversity: The Magic of Not Giving Attention to Your Problems - How to Make Disturbing Factors Absent If You Can't Control Them!

I was complaining that I had no shoes until I met a man who had no feet. - Confucius.

Have you seen personalities who have grown to become the world's best even if they had nothing and they were immensely struggling with a lot of problems that can't be avoided? Affirmative, we are talking about **Shah Rukh Khan, the world's famous Bollywood actor who came from room number 205 to a become King Khan with his intense dedication, love & hard work.** *Most problems are just perspective. The things that feel like problems to you are the* *opportunity to someone else. Damn true.* We create problems on how we perceive things. You know, most disturbing people have more problems along with their low aimed goals. People with great goals don't bother about problems because they genuinely want to succeed. Ultimately, we are creating more problems and then trying solving it instead of knowing whether to know even these problems are really relevant or not. Also, people perceive most problems as big and then try opposing them and that disturbs them for so long. ***Suppose if we lock two different personalities in a dark room that has no light, the result would be too different.*** Under this situation, one person has a good mind controlling power and the other has a disturbing mind. Now, both have to find a way to the exit in the darkness. On the first hand, the disturbing man will blame the darkness for not moving ahead with fear and finding the way while the other one can meditate and stop blaming the darkness and move slowly to find the way. Here darkness is a problem and it could be eliminated easily by his perspective and courage that's why we previously said, ***problems are just perspective.*** Some people are blaming for getting the same kind of food every day while some don't even have food. Some are dancing bare feet while some are blaming their shoes for not dancing properly. Now, when you see less problems, you can focus extremely well on your goal or in other way, when you focus on your goals well, you would see less problems because now that goal would become more significant for you.

Alexander the great pleaded, 'Through every generation of the human race there had been a constant war, a war with fear.' We feel fear is stupid. Regrets give more pain than failure. Only the most disturbing people want everything perfect;

because instead of finding themselves and seeing less problems, they see more problems in this world, the irrelevant ones and then try to make it good. ***Perfection is stupid.*** It's significant, the struggle and fear you are facing for today's problems will not be a problem for you tomorrow. Humans are very flexible and they accept it as they get problems. Every day, they want delicious food but if they get nothing the next day, they would only want food to eat, not delicacies. That's the mindset & that's why I prefer to see less problems and focus only on relevant problems which deserve to be solved.

While Irresistibly Obsessed to your great goal, you may see less problems because your goal would become more significant than any other thing. Don't oppose the factors that are disturbing your discipline but exist with them calmly and maintain your discipline along with them. When we oppose problems that can't be controlled, they steal our energy, focus, peace and attention and you would habitual to get disturbed all the time and after that you would try to solve every problem that can't be solved and boom, you are stuck forever in some infinite loop. Why do you want everything to be so perfect? It's okay to be imperfect until you don't get disturbed by them.

- ***Naval Ravikant said, a fit body, a calm mind, a house full of love. These things can't be bought - they must be earned.***

- If you think your problems will matter after years, then you are living up to illusions. We usually grow up with the problems to make their loud noise absent but they never get buried. There are no problems, just perspective, just differences. See less problems and you don't have to keep it in your heart. Enjoy.

- Only the most disturbed people want perfection. They create problems, and try to solve every part so they would see less problems.

- The problems you accept in your life, you will free that part of your mind easily. Accept what you can't change until the sun rises again.

- It's damn true, *most people don't think & judge themselves as they judge others.* Are you really afraid of people's opinions? What's disturbing you for a month, people will forget about it in a moment. Don't worry about what people think & that's how you can be yourself.

- Adolf Hitler shared, 'Anyone can deal with victory. Only the mighty can bear defeat.' We feel, only with defeat we learn & try to improvise. There are rare people who work greatest even after success. He also said, 'One who wins without a problem. It is just a victory, but, one who wins with a lot of troubles, that is, "History".' Further he added, 'Think thousand times before taking a decision but after taking a decision never turn back even if you get thousands of difficulties.'

- Always try giving your reasonable energy to the tasks. If a task deserves less energy, don't try to inject more otherwise you have to sacrifice in the tasks where you really need more energy and attention.

- I have learned, the majorities of problems don't disturb us but our own endless thoughts & mindset. Problems are eternal but once you accept them, you walk towards solutions. *Accept your problems & you can eliminate them from everywhere.* Focus on your goals and you won't see unnecessary problems.

- *Bill Gates elaborated a great statement, 'Most people overestimate what they can do in one year and underestimate what they can do in ten years.'*

- Most people think, other people are disturbing us but in fact in most cases they don't. We are our own distraction because we want to get events like we want. We want to control the entire world and that's the real problem. Your level of mindset and perspective don't reach other people's minds easily and it's not your job to teach people until they want to learn. The work obsession is so greatest ever that you don't even feel the passing of a train or at that time, you don't even feel the time and get lost into another dimension. *You don't have to remove or solve problems but to shift your focus to something relevant.*

- We feel, **when suffering is not appreciated, it's not visible.** In fact, it should be beautiful. **Your tragedies of life are heroic & inspiring to others, then why can't your tragedies be heroic to your own lives too.**

- Don't care about what people think. Think about what you think about yourself. Ralph Waldo Emerson voiced, 'To be great, is to be misunderstood.' Your duty isn't to convince others that you are great.

- **Marcus Aurelius said in his book, Meditations, 'You have power over your mind - not outside events. Realize this, & you will find strength.'**

- In focus, you forget about pleasure and pain. May be the best way to hide everything is to focus on what you love.

- The men who were complaining of the harsh sun rays in summer are now begging for them in the winter. We are clever. To be in power, you have to tackle both the weather peacefully.

I'm free and that is why I am lost. - Franz Kafka.

Unless your work gives you trouble, it is no good. - Pablo Picasso.

Normality is a paved road; it is comfortable to walk, but no flowers grow. - Vincent Van Gogh.

This is my last message to you: in sorrow, seek happiness. - Fyodor Dostoevsky.

Strategy 10

Dopamine Hacks - How to Train your Mind & Thriving Even in the Worst Situations of Life

Purpose of the Strategy: How to prepare yourself for the world's class work - How to feel self-accomplished with your work - Train your mind to remember everything you want!

I think it's possible for ordinary people to choose to be extraordinary. - Elon Musk

Train your mind. Discipline is pure practice. Change is eternal. Taste the pleasure of good habits to hack your dopamine. Watch your entire day of thoughts. Fear is stupid. Your mind is wood. Destiny is what we make it.

7 years ago, I wrote a quote, 'There's nothing like destiny in this world. It's just the human perspective to make themselves satisfied.' If you find a 45-year-old man still handsome, fit and charming, he has really worked on it whether it was his habit, discipline or obsession. Nothing is random in this world. Why people aren't extremely conscious of knowing that they are capable of doing anything they want. That's the power of training our minds. *I'm not a great writer but for me, I'm better than I used to be. I teach myself a lot. That's practice.* With some pleasure of dopamine hormone, I have been tasting the pleasure of good habits.

Whether he was Nikola Tesla, Diogenes, Alexander the Great, Merilyn Monroe or Ralph Waldo Emerson, they all chose to become what they wanted. ***Diogenes depicted, 'Time is the most valuable thing that a man can spend.'*** We know, we would never get this day back again. So, it should be lived as we want. You can still control your destiny and prepare and train yourself for world class work, whether you want to accomplish your work on time, focus on health, gain wealth or have a great relationship with people but you have to be super conscious to know what you are really doing. Time is the only god and it never comes back, ever.

You know, ***Aristotle who was the father of logic, was the private tutor of Alexander the great.*** It's damn significant who is teaching you because when you believe in your mentor honestly, you frame yourself honestly as they teach you. And it's astonishing to know, ***Plato was the teacher of Aristotle; and Socrates the teacher of Plato. Was this a coincidence?*** No, absolutely not. They all chose the wisest teacher from the lining. Above all, I really admired the line of Plato, 'Truth is the beginning of every good to the gods, and of every good to man.' We feel, good deeds are evidence of a super conscious state of mind. If someone is looking unfit at a young age then it's his fault for not taking care of his body. It's not body shaming but truth. The world-famous Hollywood classic actress of all time, Merilyn Monroe was so gorgeous because of her attention to diet. Articles say, she had a strict skincare routine even though there is still a lot of debate on her personal hygiene but she had maintained a healthy life style. She regularly cleanses, exfoliates and moisturizes her classic physique. After all, her sensuousness, vulnerability and innocence made her beautiful.

The first & best victory is to conquer self. - Plato.

Now, a great question, how to train your mind and prepare yourself for world class work! After analysing deep, researching and observing, we have created a list that will assist you to become world class and make you super conscious of everything:

- Always Remember, your mind is wood. Burn it right to get the coal otherwise the ash. Balance the thoughts in your mind well and be flexible with them. Don't be too rigid.

- *Stuck your mind to the goal that every time you are free, your mind makes you remember it.* Practice this for long until this becomes easy for you. Don't let your mind roam in the way it wants.

- ***Procrastination makes us feel guilty.*** If you ever feel you want to procrastinate, change your mind suddenly and do the opposite and you will learn, you will get more power than on actual discipline. We get more dopamine when we are expecting less and do it even with the less probability.

- ***Trust me, you don't have to remove bad habits.*** Just exist with them but try getting addicted to the pleasure of good habits & you will find highest pleasure in the long run with great feel. At one time, I was addicted to drinking milk tea but instead of eliminating it, I started to drink green tea in the evening. *When I found I was feeling good with green tea then I automatically hated the milk tea in the evening and now I rarely drink milk tea because now I'm conscious of the pleasure of the good habits on my health.* This looks simple but brilliant. Also, I drink rose tea, black tea, white peony tea, lavender tea and various flowers tea after I got great results. After adopting good habits, you may feel guilty when you try bad habits next time. Taste the pleasure of great habits and you will automatically hate the bad habits. Great habits are pleasurable in the long run. Be patient.

   - *How intelligent we are but we live well only in laughter and stupidity.* Do you really make your life exciting by yourself? We don't get enjoyment but we create it. Shock yourself. The only abnormality in our lives is to remain normal. Stay abnormal.

   - Always try to excite yourself to remain energetic and excite the audience too.

   - It's fortunate, if you are capable of distinguishing between right and wrong instead of choosing your favourites. And you have to learn, when you choose the right, or as soon as you protect yourself from the wrong when you learn about it, the wrong will betray & curse you more.

   - *A leader is the king. You are the leader.* Alexander the great said, 'I'm not afraid of an army of lions led by a sheep; I am afraid of an army of sheep led by a lion.'

   - *In sadness, be the first one to crack a joke and it will flow away.*

   - *Adolf Hitler observed, 'If you don't like a rule, just follow it. Reach to the top and change the rule.'*

- If you can't entertain yourself, go on focusing on something you love. That's the best way to cheat time.

- In an article, we read, **Haruki Murakami** follows an intense routine from six months to a year and that really requires a good amount of mental and physical strength. Its damn true physical strength is as necessary as artistic sensitivity.

- There's a *Bill Gates mentality: Optimism is power but don't confuse them with blind optimism. Optimism should be calculated.*

- Always take pleasure in what you have done so far too. *Marie Curie expressed, 'One never notices what has been done; one can only see what remains to be done.'*

- *There's a Golden Rule. Whatever you want, don't seek it.* If you want peace, don't seek it because when you focus on it, it will fade away. Focus on combined efforts and you will get it even without asking for it. Franz Kafka said, 'He who seeks doesn't find, but he who does not seek will be found.'

- *Vincent Van Gogh voiced, 'What would life be if we had no courage to attempt anything.'* He also depicted, Let's not forget that the little emotions are the great captains of our lives & we obey them without realising it.'

- Try to find interstices. When you feel you can't work, find a little more time, add some efforts & do a little as an addition & you will get more motivation and a sense of accomplishment.

- *The mind is everything; what you think you become. -* Socrates. *Also, he clarified, 'We cannot live better than in seeking to become better. The same lines were said by Franz Kafka in different form. He also mentioned, 'Only the extremely ignorant or the extremely intelligent can resist change.' Also, Confucius uttered the same thing in different form, 'Only the wisest & stupidest of men never change.'*

- As we all are directing our lives and, in that relevance, Confucius shared, 'The man who thinks he can and the man who thinks he can't both are right.'

- When you want to do more & don't take action, you will think endlessly. Always try your best to take action. That's visible.

- ***Winning is overrated. Success is overrated. Love and self-satisfaction are extremely underrated.***

- Don't over plan. Don't plan above your capabilities and energy. Plan right & then do slightly more than you actually planned. That's a beautiful satisfaction.

- When you have nothing to do, do what you love the most like Vincent Van Gogh. He's the perfect instance of doing what you truly love even if no one cares.

To the mind that is still, the whole universe surrenders. - Lao Tzu. He also added, stop thinking and end your problem.

To improve is to change; to be perfect is to change often. - Winston Churchill.

The universe does not behave according to our pre conceived ideas. It continues to surprise us. - Stephen Hawking.

Strategy 11

Storytelling Mastery: The Proficiency of Storytelling - You are deciding your destiny - What are you telling yourself?

Purpose of the Strategy: How Discipline is storytelling to yourself & others - How to be an extremely valuable asset. - Beware of what great story you are telling yourself - The Power of confidence and courage in your own story – How to treat the world's toughest task damn easy - How tough you are seeing in your mind – Why madness is necessary to get the impossible.

Bury the body & don't build any monument. Keep my hands out so the people know the one who won the world had nothing in hand when he

died. - *Alexander the Great Last words.*

Storytelling is powerful. It's effective & memorable. It's eternal even if it's simple. It's a courage to self. People don't remember the words but the tales. History remembers the great storytellers whether you are a writer or a businessman. We all are storytellers in different forms. *A great story to self is relevant before we serve a soothing story to others.*

The world remembers the storytelling, not the words. Whether it was Diogenes or Alexander the Great, they both told themselves a different story to win as they wanted. If Diogenes wanted to be a cynic, it was his choice of story to himself and that's how he lived much better. Alexander the Great told himself in his earlier years that he would win the entire world and become greatest and that was his choice. *Diogenes and Alexander both were opposite personalities but they both hold strong stories that give them power and strength in living.* No one was in guilt while living and that's why it's significant what you actually think about yourself and tell what great story to your soul. If it's acceptable to you, it can be brilliant. You can live well and that's all right & even it may not be best. Even if Nikola Tesla built the AC motor, he really wanted to. The beginning of a greatest work builds with the strong story even whether its onspiring or not. Would you still remember Vincent Van Gogh as a great painter if he was super rich in his time or whether he would tell himself the story of doing what he wanted. Every circumstance we face builds a story. *So, instead of blaming the events, we should make our tale strong and that can push us very well.*

Every greatest invention was invented out of someone's madness. ***Adolf Dassler stated, 'Coming to work every day as if it was the first time. This will prevent you from being blinded by routine.'*** We feel, we are all building our fortune and destiny with what we really seek from our hearts. Don't you know about Adolf Dassler? He was a passionate person and had a great story of creativity. *Affirmative, he's the founder of ADIDAS along with his younger brother Rudolf Dassler who later became PUMA's founder.* Before ADIDAS, there were rare sports brands, so Adolf Dassler realised the individual needs of every sport, accumulated courage and after that the same idea became the backbone of the future company. Initially, ADIDAS made handmade shoes which were personally made by Adolf himself. Their first success came at the 1928 Olympics in Amsterdam when Adolf Dassler gave a pair of spiked tracked shoes to German runner ***Lina Radke***. Also, it was the first-time women had been allowed in the 800m distance and fortunately she won the race with a world record time. And after that in an incident when a black American athlete ***Jesse Owens*** lost his track shoes on the way to the game in Berlin, Adolf Dassler introduced shoes to try out and he also won four gold medals & after that he became the brand ambassador of the Company, ADIDAS. The company was always ready to make history. *They were ready and prepared till the opportunities knocked and then they seized them very well.*

It's astounding to know, we all are telling stories to ourselves and that's what we actually become. Adidas once started in a washroom where the first electricity room was prepared and now, they have conquered the entire world. They mentioned some inspiring words on their website, "*We've done our best for the best. We've improved & grown. Looking ahead to the future, always remembering where we came from. This is our story.*"

- In your life, you have to begin something to know how much you love it. You won't know until you separate that task from your life.

- Most people don't know; Steve Jobs literally had a fear of failure in his life. He never wanted to get failed, so in that fear he started seeking perfection in his work, so he would never ever fail and if any company is a pure perfectionist then Apple Inc is the one. *Steve Jobs leadership style is world famous and often criticized harshly. He was ruthless when it came to time and details.* He was known as a *frame fucker* because he had an eye for details and checked everything frame by frame and often, he denied many things without even giving how to correct it. He just denied it. Also, he was a fast decision maker even with eye catching details. That's his great story. He knew what he wanted and he did everything very well.

- Pay attention to your work because your work inspires you first to do the best.

- To build a lot of courage, tell yourself this every day: Don't ever fear with a little to lose but take risks to grab the opportunities. *Opportunities and days once gone, they don't come back. Remember that.*

- *A leader is the first employee of the company and the other employees follow him well.* Even Elon Musk is super intelligent and richest person in the world, he himself does more work and is heavily involved in the design and engineering process at Tesla and SpaceX. Don't ever care about the throne. Are you the king?

- The world belongs to the strongest & the courageous people who have the capability to tell great stories to themselves. There are enough intelligent people on the planet.

- If you love something from your heart & you don't find the way. Go with courage & whether you will see the way ahead or make one.

- *Martin Luther King Jr. stated, Faith is taking the first step even when you don't see the whole staircase and taking active participation in what you want from your life & lead well.*

- For being smart and wise, be the last person to speak, till then add on & calculate every speaker's words.

- I have learned, how you are talking with yourself is how far you will go because if you can't convince yourself for the fire in your heart, no one will ever.

- There's always a cost to being mad about something you love. Vincent Van Gogh was an introvert avoiding social needs & suffering from depression and anxiety. *You can't be everywhere in your obsession.*

- *Conscience is a man's compass. - Vincent Van Gogh.*

- If you want to learn about great storytelling to others and yourself and want to be irresistibly obsessed with what you really love then **Alfred Hitchcock** is the right damn personality. He understood the significance of visual storytelling. Also, he was an obsessed film maker who was focused on making great cinema with much observed details, choosing the right characters, plot, and extreme details and that's how he created God like films. *We believe everything* *is great storytelling along with deep art. People are really fascinated by it truly.*

Also, there was a case during the filming of '*The 39 Steps*' *movie in which Alfred Hitchcock handcuffed two leads together in a scene and pretended he had lost the key.* The actors were chained and they didn't know about that they were getting filmed during that chaos and finally a great shot captured while no one knew he already had a key in his coat. After Alfred Hitchcock explained he did it because he wanted to shoot a great scene through naturality and great chemistry.

- If you fear being bold, different and creative then you will become like the same as everyone else but to be great, you should build the courage to stand out. **Difference is not the curse but uniqueness.**

- Plato advised, the harder you work, the luckier you get. Also, courage is knowing what not to fear.

- Ralph Waldo Emerson voiced, 'A hero is no braver than an ordinary man, but he is braver five minutes longer.' Stick to what you love and you will succeed effortlessly.

It's a reminder that, *Irresistible Obsession book is a journey to know your own soul, practicing your mindset, going deep inside your potential and preparing yourself for the best. This book isn't focused on depicting what to do but it will prepare you to achieve the impossible.*

It's always more difficult to fight against faith than to fight against knowledge. - Adolf Hitler.

Be nice to nerds. Chances are you'll end up working for one. - Bill Gates.

Those who tell the stories rule society. - Plato.

Strategy 12

The Fuel of Focusing on One by Swami Vivekananda

Purpose of the Strategy: The Power of Minimalisation - The Power & Art of doing the only thing - Digital Detoxification: Doing it in the right way!

Take up one idea. Make that one idea your life - think of it, dream of it, live on that idea. Let the brain, muscles, nerves, every part of your body be full of that idea and just leave every other idea alone. This is the way to success. - Swami Vivekananda.

I have heard a statement many times, **'When I drink water, I only drink water and nothing else.'** I don't think about anything else at that time. I get entirely involved to feel the pleasure of the moment and I'm truly grateful to be focused.' Multitasking is overrated. It gives you training to focus on a lot at one time and divides your energy and makes you feel confused. Everything is purely practice and we are giving wrong training to our own minds with multitasking. Hence, if you want to divide your energy into many tasks at a time then you would feel uneasy when you really want to do a sole thing.

Of course, I can give you the best instance. These days adults don't eat only but eating has become a side activity. They want to enjoy shows while eating. So, every time we find a person who is only eating without doing nothing else then he looks like fools to everyone else because he tries to adopt right what most people aren't doing. Look, how alone he is! No, we have evolved backwards and these stupid habits are preparing for doing a lot and consuming too much energy at a point in time. We mentioned earlier in almost all chapters, focus is meditation and when we do many things at a time, we prepare bad habits to do many things at a time. Here, in doing many things, we lose too much energy because we aren't focusing on one and stressing on many. It consumes us faster than a sole task and eats up our true potential. Secondly, your work should enhance your emotional and mental energy. Of course, you can be physically exhausted but mentally healthy and these days, people are more mentally tired than physically. That's insanely dangerous.

Steve Jobs understands, 'Innovation is saying no to a thousand things.' *It's better we take two good life changing decisions than hundred decisions that aren't of no use.* By focusing on one, we can get lost into the right work with high potential, may get deep with simplicity but you will make it close to perfect. It's damn true, focus comes from doing only a task at a time but we are becoming habitual of doing many tasks at a time and it's happening because we want to succeed as fast as we can and, in that urge, we are now open to the best things of this world. Success makes us crazy to get our goals fast but the aim of success is to enjoy the journey. If the journey is painful, success is bullshit. Also, the digital world has destroyed us in many ways. It was designed like that to occupy us while playing with our emotions, attention and interests. So, even in tiredness we are getting more consumed. We should know when to stop getting involved in them. ***Emotions are a dangerous part of human beings and of course, we are getting served with a lot of emotions at a time which is hampering our own stability.*** Do you know why people become monks because they want to get rid of everything but if you want to get rid of something even while being in the course of life then you can easily do it by practice. Practice doing one thing at a time; only one and you will succeed effortlessly without getting exhausted.

- ***Don't be a multitasker but focus on one task at a time to bring out your best.***

- Reading is a great activity to focus on. It makes me realise, I know nothing. I still need to walk more & traveling the entire world with books in my hands.

- The internet has destroyed us well in the course of time to steal our focus, consume our emotions, and bring a drastic habit to doing many tasks at a time.

- ***Marie Curie is known as the master of simplification.*** She chose to focus on one or two projects at a time rather than trying to accomplish multiple tasks simultaneously. She was known for strict work routine and kept set aside everything to do research & avoid distractions to bring out her best. It reflects her diligent work ethic and sometimes she even neglected food and sleep to study. That's a pure healthy obsession. It reflects her character traits like she was loving what she was doing, utilizing her high intelligence with proper focus and had strong conviction to provide something good to humanity.

- If we followed the simple rules of ancient people, we would be happy because they do things slowly rather than rushing. ***The purpose of work is primarily to enjoy the process without rushing. In rushing, we miss the true details of the Masterpiece.***

- I will not give you long lectures on ***Digital Detoxification but recommend you to get involved where you feel energetic after that.*** If you feel consumed after doing something, it's not right. That's it. When you accomplish the right task, you will be happy, not exhausted. We are not here to get consumed with anything. Choose wisely whether it's people, tasks or the digital world. Ancient people were enjoying the work while we try accomplishing the work & get exhausted in the process. That's pure bullshit.

- Just choose one and do the best of this world and remember, don't carry gadgets around you.

If you try to do much, you will not conquer anything. - Confucius.

Strategy 13

The Ruthless Schedule: Why Do You Have to Be Clever to Be Obsessed with Your Loving Work - How to Protect Your Energy and Time for The Right Work

Great things are not done by impulse, but by a series of small things brought together. - Vincent Van Gogh.

If you want to say yes to yourself then trust me, you will have to piss a lot of people in your life. If you want to say yes to others, you have to say no to yourself and every second person can consume you even without reaching you. It doesn't mean we don't have time for our work but we don't actually prioritize our time. Before prioritizing, you may not even have time to accomplish your everyday tasks but after analysing and prioritizing every moment, you will have a lot of time even after accomplishing what you want, you may stiff left with some time too. That's the power of knowing yourself that with whom you will share your energy. That's the super conscious state of humans.

Ruthless, affirmative, you have to be extremely ruthless about your vision and schedule otherwise you would always have a long list of pending work till your last breath. If you want to keep everyone happy, you can skip this chapter because you will seriously piss a lot of people including your family members, friends or even your partner if they aren't understandable carefully. Apart from every relationship, helping people for pleasing, enjoying and participating in social chores, we should have a great goal which should be directly interlinked with our soul satisfaction and when we don't do it, we may feel disappointed and dissatisfied. It may or may not be a matter to anybody else but only to you. We all are perceiving differently and it's damn okay but if you are seeing a genius way then it's your responsibility & hard work to taste it. Why do people have to care about your time? People are rude when it comes to expectations and they want everything to work as they want. Your friends expect a lot of time with you. Your partner also expects the same. Of course, work life balance is significant but your time is limited and you can't be everywhere. Your energy is significant so you have to inject your energy in your loving areas.

Steve Jobs character depicted a ruthless behaviour that can be learned when we are irresistibly obsessed with our vision:

A. Be rude & straightforward for what you want. Don't ever linger and roundabout even if you have to be blunt, be one. Don't please people & be professional with your work even if you are working with your close friend.

B. Focus on perfection if it's possible. Perfection is possible if you pay attention to the details.

C. Try to motivate your people even if you are failing. Rise from the ashes.

D. Don't involve more people in you work but talent only. A few talented people can beat the entire universe.

E. Take instant hard action before you get exhausted with its planning.

F. Prioritize Ruthlessly: Be ruthless with your goals otherwise you will entertain every second person in your life.

G. Deciding what not to do is as important as deciding what to do. - Steve Jobs.

H. During an annual internship program, Steve Jobs even scolded interns for asking the stupid questions too.

After perceiving, we have concluded a few tips that can assist you to prioritize ruthlessly:

- If your task is significant and you get high satisfaction from it, do it frequently and don't ever avoid it in any case. It's precious.

- **Prioritize otherwise you will become everyone's slaves.** Good energies are often in high demand and people want to be around them. There will always be a confusion of whether you want to be with your work or with the people to expand your energy. Choose wisely.

- ***Surround yourself with people who understand you extremely well; who are aware of your goals.*** People who don't have extreme goals try to find people who can give them great feelings in this lethargic world. Beware carefully.

- Put significant tasks as vital and everything else is a distraction. Make a sense of urgency in a good way. Your time is limited.

- If you are a highly obsessed person with your work then as soon as you get energetic, attack your work before you get consumed anywhere else. Be extremely close to your workplace or office setup, so you can reach it anytime you want. Steve Jobs usually begins work at home & then goes to the office to inject his most energy to the right tasks.

- Just like Steve Jobs, Elon Musk, Pablo Picasso or Marie Curie, they all were ruthless about their time even though they pissed a lot of people in their lives.

- You know, when you prioritize your time, people will call you selfish or cruel & that's okay. It's your own life. You are allowed to work on your vision, anyway.

- Even Alexander the Great who never got defeated in his entire life had time to read the books. He was an avid reader of the great classics, truly fond of Iliad written by Homer and the Odyssey. He considered the Iliad a perfect portable treasure of all military virtue & knowledge.

- It was argued that Alexander the Great was a big drinker. Although we all are genius in our own attributes & skills but may get collapsed by some of the negative reasons. Remember, even a genius can be collapsed for a silly reason. *Be protective & analyse yourself cautiously and consistently.*

- Create urgency in your work but never hurry in the work you love.

- Merilyn Monroe was a well-read woman, perfectly impressive. At the time of her death, she owned more than 400 volumes, including several first editions.

Until you achieve your everyday goals, don't get consumed anywhere else.

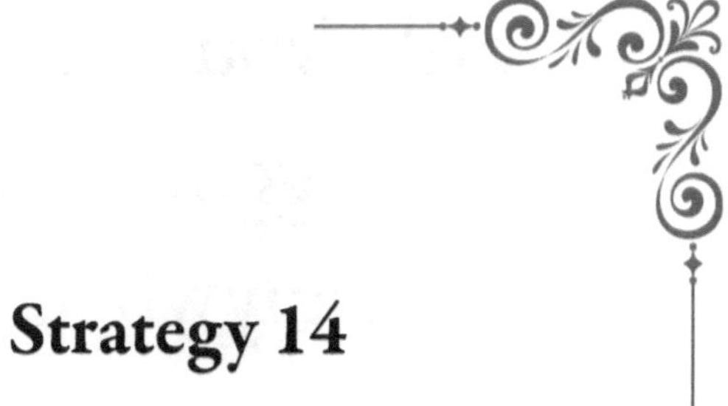

Strategy 14

The True Horsepower of Doing Practice - Practice, Practice, Practice, & Practice Until You Become the Person You Really Love

Purpose of the Strategy: Build & Practice the skills - How to become the master of Skills: - What if you are zero in what you really love?

You can get better at almost anything if you put effort into it. - Steve Jobs.

Genius is overrated. Interest and curiosity are underrated. Most people become successful because they wanted to be. Some people are born with what they find interesting & It becomes easy for them to succeed in that while some people have zero skills in what they love, so they become curious and develop into the person they want but people call them genius!

Do you know about Dyson company? Of course, now we are aware of Dyson which is famous for its marvellous air purifiers. *The founder of Dyson, Sir James Dyson failed 5,216* *times with the prototype of a bagless vacuum cleaner but now has a net worth of $4.5 trillion.* Also, likewise, once *Thomas Elva Edison* told by his teachers that he was too slow to learn anything. His teachers thought he was very slow but Edison later quoted, *'I have not failed 10,000 times. I've successfully found 10,000 ways that will not work.'* So, when people say, 'I did it because I'm a genius, I laugh!' I have been seeing highly intelligent people who are full of potential and doing nothing; and curious average people who have beaten them with curiosity and consistent practice. Edison was always a curious boy, usually self-taught and he loved to read books. *He even did 50,000 experiments to make practical & feasible alkaline batteries. It's a great depiction of a great attitude and persistence.*

We think, we try, we fail and we learn. Some have great capabilities to reach their goals swiftly while some take a few more tries to reach the same goal because we all are built differently; the biological brains and genes are different but curiosity, attentiveness, interest, skills and practice can be built with an irresistible obsession with our goal. When you try after learning from mistakes and experience, you enhance the process and then you can reach your best.

On failure, Walt Disney sounded, 'I think it's important to have a good hard failure when you're young... because it makes you kind of aware of what happens to you. Because of it I've never had any fear in my whole life when we've been near collapse & all of that, I've never been afraid.'

How to do marvellous practice to become your own best! We have made some great bullet points that will make you super conscious of what you have to do ahead with your obsession:

- First, always try to keep upgrading your skills even if your work fails because skills increase when you practice & even after you get failed in your 99th, *may be your fortune is in your 100th work* & after that you may realise, you weren't even failed but till that time you weren't formed into the person that can make you successful. You will fail more or less but to become skilful, build the tough resilience to fail.

- *A genius can also be failed if he doesn't work honest enough.* A talented man can be failed without practice but a man who practices continuously becomes the person he wants & he can even do intense practice in the work he loves because that's how he can tackle the failures. When you are about to climb the mountain, don't get afraid of falling because in the process of climbing, you will build the courage to see the view without fear as soon as you start your journey. Start your journey, dear. *Genius is overrated. You can even bring down the mountain or split it in half with your hard work efforts, obsession and practice.*

- *Perfection comes in your work when you break down your work into the details & focus on every atom carefully & clearly.* Understand before proceeding. Perfection is when you do it again and again with improvisation, learning, deep intensity and more interest.

- You know, passionate people work more than job holders. It's known as hyper productivity, and maybe they work 80-100 hours a week.

- Always try to push yourself to the impossible, so you can build the skills to become that person. Trust me, you can be anyone you want. It's up to you.

- *When you are yourself, you become perfect. When you try to be something else, you have to try hard.* Just be yourself and the universe will fall into your place.

- *Marie Curie voiced, 'I was taught that the way of progress was never Swift nor easy. It always takes time.'* She also taught, 'Humanity needs both practical men and dreamers. If you are honest with yourself while working, you are already winning.'

- In order to learn something, you have to do that thing. There's no other way. Vincent Van Gogh elaborated, 'I've just kept on ceaselessly painting in order to learn painting.'

- *A career born in public - Talent in Privacy. - Merilyn Monroe.*

- I have learned from Alfred Hitchcock style that if you want a great perfection in your work, treat all your factors like cattle otherwise the sense of perfection would get lost with the adjustments. If you have a great vision and you are sure of it then try leading your team like cattle. It's looking like a harsh way but that's the way to implement your vision.

- *Work like there's no tomorrow. Train, strive. Really train and cultivate your talent to the highest degree. - Michael Jackson.*

- Getting dissatisfied with your work is the best way to know you want improvement.

- I am always doing that which I cannot do, in order that I may learn how to do it. - Pablo Picasso.

- Also, it's a case too; sometimes don't seek perfection while working on the best but progress. That will prevent procrastination, laziness and help you to gain confidence while working and also self-accomplishment. Do your work greatly but don't pressurize yourself otherwise you will lose the essence.

- Intelligence, consciousness, knowledge and wisdom wash away if we don't practice it in real life. You have to live goodness well at all times.

- ***Socrates shared, 'Employ your time in improving yourself by other men's writings so that you shall come easily by what others have laboured hard for.'***

- Sometimes you don't have the skills for what you truly love but you can also build while loving them. Practice until you become a pro and curious and then you will automatically become more obsessed with bringing out the best.

- Better a diamond with a flaw than a pebble without. - Confucius. Also, he voiced, 'If you make a mistake and do not correct it, this is called a mistake.'

- Unless you try to do something beyond what you have already mastered, you will never grow. - Ralph Waldo Emerson.

Before we end this chapter, we want to elaborate a few scientific proven rules. The first one is the ***10,000 hours rule that was taken from Malcolm Gladwell's book. It depicts that an intentional practice of 10,000 hours is required to master complex skills and materials.*** It clarifies, practice is the essence of a genius. 10,000 hours of practice is often known as the magic number of greatness and it's regardless of a person's natural aptitude. So, there's nothing like being genius. Like, if you carried out 80 hours of work a week, it would take around 2.6 years to master great skills. History says, *Michael Jackson* *went through this 10,000-hour rule of dancing mastery. He used 18 hours to dance and rehearse a day and took around 556 days which is less than 2 years; mind boggling.* There's a fun fact, Michael Jackson always wore a pair of socks to hide his feet, which was his pure magic, maybe they were deformed due to intense practice.

Affirmative, there's another **Kaufman's 20 hours rule which says a person can learn any new skill by dedicating 20 hours of planned practice time to that skill. Good luck.**

Adolf Dassler depicted, 'Never be satisfied with your accomplishments; always continue to learn.'

The greatest enemy of knowledge is not ignorance, it is the illusion of knowledge. - Stephen Hawking.

Have no fear of perfection; you will never reach it. - Marie Curie.

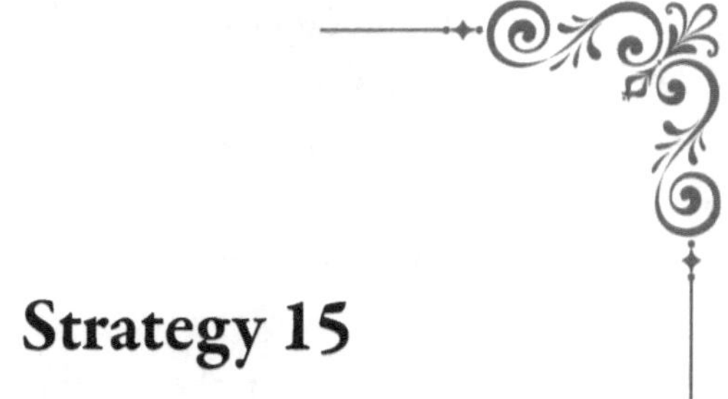

Strategy 15

Cheat the Time: How to Focus for Long & Not Knowing the Passing of Time

Purpose of the Strategy: How to feel less exhausted - Stay less exhausted by momentary focus - Save your energy-Save your day - How many senses you are using at a time!

Time is an illusion. Almost all people have enough time to shake the world but what truly matters is how we are utilizing our energy.

What would happen if Pablo Picasso started to write books instead of painting or Marilyn Monroe became director instead of an actress or Vincent Van Gogh started dancing instead of painting? Of course, that's a deadly combination of struggling and expanding too much energy to bring out nothing even after doing hard work. Hard work isn't bad but there's always something in which we are flawless, effortless and do it without too much energy and pain while for the same work, some people would get consumed before time. Almost every young fella is struggling because they all are running towards the career which was planted in front of us. See, we always had a limited career choice instead of thinking out of the box and that's because we don't want to get failed. We all want surety of success, so we choose something that has high chance of success. It doesn't mean we want to be successful but we don't really have the capability to handle failures so, silently, we choose a tough path where we become successful soon and get money but in the long run, it consumes us till the end. Along with money, why people don't understand we also have to live a great life and for it, we need to create immense energy and feel great every moment with something & even without any expectations from it. That's pure love. Suppose if you are getting consumed where you don't want to, you will lose your charm and endlessly the money would be useless.

The art of cheating time elaborates to focus on your most loving work and try making livelihood with it and trust me, you will be happier because maybe you have less or more positive results in the long run but your satisfaction will always be high after working on it. People who work on the tasks that don't belong to them are usually stressed out easily and can't work for too long because they are working with efforts; and endlessly, they get exhausted while the person who is loving his work can do more even without knowing the passing of time. If you can cheat on time, you can save your energy and still be energetic after doing a lot of work. It's all about the senses. In focus, we forget about everything even ourselves and that slows down our consumption of energy. Writers, painters, or dancers play for too long because of that reason and even sports players feel easy because they love it. The play can be a little physically exhausted but not mentally tiring and here people are getting mentally tired while carrying out the work.

You know, I want to skip this chapter but still felt it relevant to share some information with you. It's not based on much research but will take you far in life.

Also, it really matters how many senses you use while carrying out your tasks. In focus, we forget about our senses and become less sensitive to hearing or speaking and that tremendously saves our energy. *If you have ever observed, artistic people have great routines and they work for too long and that may look exhausting to other people but trust me they all save their energy, enjoy and use their energy wisely in the right tasks. That's all.*

Strategy 16

Heart or Mind: Which One to Follow in Your Work & Life - The Strength of Intuition and Loving People in The Right Way & Lead Your Crucial Life Decisions!

What is done in love is done well. - Vincent Van Gogh.

A Constant War, what to follow in life; *Love or Intelligence! Intelligence is ruling the living world but hearts are creating the eternal history of all time.* Where everyone is appreciating intelligence in this world then how someone can be heartful in this selfish world! That's arduous.

The world's richest man & founder of Amazon Inc. Jeff Bezos once clarified, he took most of the great life decisions by following his heart, gut feelings & emotions. It's definitely an astounding thing when a richest man suggests us to make great decisions by our intuitions and of course, that's true because ultimately, we are heart and soul, not intelligence. We all make great decisions by the patterns of our intuitions and I strongly believe this too. Irresistible Obsession is particularly latent in our heart. Intelligence pushes us but the heart pulls us. Do you know the reason why Japanese people live longer? Because they aren't self-centred and seek happiness. They don't only believe in work life but in caring people. It's true, we all want to love people so we can feel better. *In Japanese culture, their idea is to serve love, build a great loving community and pray for the team honestly. Social togetherness is the most significant element that is missing in the 21st century people.*

Japanese people often follow a concept, *Altruism*, that depicts the facts of caring about the needs & happiness of other people than their own. It's not self-avoiding but self-serving. It's very much embedded in their culture and helps in releasing dopamine in their brains. It's true, when we serve others, we grow love within ourselves. It's like, if you do something for others, it would benefit you too.

We feel, emotions are the deep chamber to create the masterpieces. People don't remember intelligence but love for a long time. Intelligence usually evolves with human's upgradation but hearts still remain constant and loving. Even if you want to convince or hypnotize an intelligent man, you should focus on winning his emotions and you are already there. Irresistible Obsession depicts how the world's best personalities have become immortal because they are still winning more hearts than minds. People still have the soft side for Nikola Tesla and Vincent Van Gogh. When people perceive Vincent Van Gogh paintings, they wonder how difficult and beautiful was for him & at the same time. It's all the heartful emotions of people. Whether it was Franz Kafka, people still admire the pain he took his entire life. So, a great story is formed with emotions and love. Intelligence is always rising but how would you win the intelligent man, by your love.

Now, we have designed a great list of loving tips from the bottom of our heart that can be easily understood and implemented in a pure way:

- You bring out your best when you really do something with your heart, not your intelligence.

- The question of life is not who will remember us later but who is remembering us when we are alive because even if one day, we wouldn't be here then what's the use of love. The right time to feel great is the present moment because if you don't feel like dancing today while doing your work, you are doing something against your heart and soul.

- Create the most impossible thing with your heart even if it's ahead of time and even if no one understands it because there comes be a day when someone who will understand your heart; there's always someone to understand you, my dear.

- You know, ***Nikola Tesla never married but he had a bizarre passion for pigeon puzzling.*** He was damn passionate about his work and just because he remained single. He was definitely a private person but he fell in love with a very special white pigeon that visited him regularly & he voiced heartily, *'I love that pigeon as a man loves a woman, & she loved me.' We feel, it's not the love you make. It's the love you give.*

- And when your heart gets heavy & your mind gets ignited, you are ready for the world's best work.

- Love is the highest form of greatest ever feeling for human kind whether you are doing it with your work or someone else. What's truly difficult with mind, becomes so easy when we do it with our heart. Love makes us fly. *Charlie Chaplin conveyed, 'We think too much and feel too little.* He also elaborated, 'You need power, only when you want to do something harmful otherwise love is enough to get everything done.'

- It's damn true, most humans don't have the courage to fail, so they remain mediocre in fear but whatever we are, we should do what we really love from our hearts & everything else is a void. If money is true happiness, then give it to the man who is taking his last breaths.

- A human heart dies when he doesn't do what he loves. He would become tired if he chooses what he never wanted. You don't need more words but your heart & feelings & you will know more about what you truly love with time.

- ***Even if love is a lie, I want to live infinite lies along with it.***

- If you are super intelligent and want to laugh, do the easiest and stupidest things ever.

- To convince people, you need emotions, heart and love. Love alone is enough to do great things to establish the strongest connection in the universe. Always try to create great values and be valuable.

- ***Motivation is void and irregular. We don't need motivation to do what we already love. For great connections, love is enough. Always fulfil people's ego, magic & emotions & you can make them do anything.***

- The greatest power of the universe lies in love & that's enough. What people are seeking outside, lies within. The cure of satisfaction lies within us. In the urge for great happiness of short tenure, we lose peace. It's not about rich or poor, happy or sad or anything but how you feel within yourself. Great feeling is the biggest wealth anyone can own to fly even when no one will ever know about it.

- ***Calm is the biggest superpower. Without love, everything is a waste.*** Whatever you are, be in love. It's the most beautiful feeling in the world. Martin Luther King Jr stated, 'I have decided to stick to love. Hate is too great a burden to bear.'

- I'm really impressed by Haruki Murakami who wrote in his book, The Wind-up Bird Chronicle, 'Spend your money on the things money can buy. Spend your time on the things money can't buy.' That's simple and a masterpiece.

- Most brilliant ideas of life don't come when we chase but when we open our heart & stay natural and go with the flow. When we get connected to something we love, we get the best ideas. You know, Murakami got his first idea of a book while watching a baseball match. His first thought was 'Goodness, I want to compose a book' that voice came from his heart. That's the power of good emotions. You get a perfect intuition after understanding the subconscious parts of the patterns around you.

- ***Jeff Bezos clarified, 'One day you will understand that it's harder to be kind than clever.'***

- ***Anne Frank wrote emotions and feelings in her diary - "Who would ever think that so much went on in the soul of a young girl?" That's pure emotional pain.***

- Life is not about accomplishing but about its true beauty. Don't forget to love the beautiful things. Marie Curie conveyed, 'A man who thinks respect is in the third dimension & love in the fourth is not worth a woman's time.'

- Look you are already connected with our opinions and that's how we also connect with history and people of the past. That's the pure magic of emotions and love. Marie Curie also mentioned, 'You will find that one special love that you know is right but for some reason just doesn't last.' We feel, even if we find love for a short tenure, it's worth the entire life's wait.

- *How much* **Franz Kafka** *was in pain when he wrote, 'Milena, if a million loved you, I am one of them and if one loved you, it was me, if no one loved you then know that I am dead.'*

- When I feel & do something in love, I love life intensely & in that too, I love greatly.

- And the music in your heart decides whether you have to dance, walk, feel peace or cry. It's always your emotions; the tune in your heart that decides the intensity of your love.

- ***Michael Jackson suggested, 'To give someone a piece of your heart, is worth more than all the wealth in the world.'*** Also, he added, 'People need love. It's the most powerful emotion in the world.' We feel, it can't be a coincidence that almost all world's best personalities are inclined with emotions and heart than intelligence because love takes you very far. Intelligence takes you fast but nowhere.

- ***Pablo Picasso expressed, 'It took me four years to paint like Raphael, but a lifetime to paint like a child.' That's insanely deep. In addition, Socrates said the thing in a different form, 'An honest man is always a child.'***

- It's astonishing to know that Confucius entire philosophy was based on kindness. He stated a Golden rule that depicts, 'People should not do to others what they do not wish to be done to them.' It's purely a combination of education and self-reflection. He once said this too, 'Life is really simple but we insist on making it complicated.

The heart is the centre of intelligence, not the brain. - Aristotle.

Love is not love that alters when its alteration finds itself. They do not love those that do not show their love. - William Shakespeare.

I am seeking, I am striving, I am in it with all my heart. - Vincent Van Gogh.

Only the heart knows how to find what is precious. - Fyodor Dostoevsky.

Strategy 17

Fostering Vibrating Energy: How to Create & Work in A High Energetic Environment & Build World Class Work!

Purpose of the Strategy: The secrets of fire & obsession in your work! - How to build the greatest, powerful and positive environment - How to create the best environment for world class work!

You need great thinkers around you. Without them, you will go broke. - Adolf Dassler, the founder of ADIDAS.

I'm a writer like everyone else but I have struggled a lot for the personal space where I could feel like I'm equivalent to a dead man like *Nikola Tesla* desired his entire life. He voiced, '*I want solitude for my writing, not like a hermit, that wouldn't be enough but like a dead man.*' It's absolutely true, without deep solitude, a great work isn't possible. You can't be your best until you forget yourself so try digging for what is right. In the initial years of my writing career, I wanted my family to leave me in some deep solitude for weeks or even months so, I could wake up and directly attack the writing process instead of getting consumed somewhere else. That's the initial challenge we all face when we have a great goal but somehow, we don't reach it with our high level of energy. I feel, Haruki Murakami starts writing at 4am because writing requires a lot of concentration and you can't be lethargic low active in it otherwise you would write like playing tennis with net down. ***Writing is a pure process of penning meaningful truth than doing it in a free form. You have to be energetic, hyper active and alert otherwise you will not get the best out of yourself.*** That's going to be all kinds of work. As we wake up, we have two choices; to attack the work or enjoy some leisure time. I have learned, when we are irresistibly obsessed, we need extreme mental, emotional and physical strength to go extra for a day and it would become too difficult for other non-goal-oriented people to understand why you are in a hurry. People are selfish sometimes and they think if they are free from their work then they would consume your time too and most times it would become hard for you to say no because maybe the person who is bothering you, can be your family member or best friend.

If you are highly satisfied with your work, you should do it in any case like Vincent Van Gogh who was extremely active in his last years or Pablo Picasso who made painting even on the last day of life at the age of 91. Goal oriented people feel extremely satisfied with what they do and that's why they become irresistibly obsessed.

Steve Jobs had some marvellous habits to avoid wastage of time. Some are mentioned below:

- Steve Jobs always placed his goals and tasks in front of his eyes. You can use stickers on your work table. I also use this method and it's extremely effective to make you remember of your vital tasks. In any way, you have to remind yourself of your own goals otherwise you will get consumed somewhere else before reaching your goals.

- Steve Jobs recommended taking action when you feel most scared as it reduces stress and builds courage. It's really the great part of creating a high energetic environment.

- Always use the morning energy at the right place and immediately plus take reasonable rest too. Don't stuff your morning mind with too much burden of what you have to do the entire day.

- Steve Jobs felt early hours of days are most productive or you can also try Jeff Bezos Puttering Method which we mentioned in one of our chapters to save your energy.

- If you want to generate ideas or do brainstorming then morning time is the best time.

- Whatever happens, always be fearless and focused.

- Steve Jobs taught us to hire or be with people who guide us what we actually have to do. He also suggested us to pay attention to details if you want perfection and intense work.

- Apple Inc. created products that most people almost lick while using it. They don't create products but value, art and hyper innovation. Recently Apple vision pro is the best instance in which they are creating demands for the products we don't even need but after perceiving we all want it. They feel, every great product is the result of a great art.

- Steve Jobs created products of such a high standard that people are unable finding its substitute. Once you join the Apple ecosystem, you are already a loyal customer.

- Many articles clarified, Steve Jobs had the fascination of Zen Buddhism which is focused on teaching, practice and enlightenment.

Likewise, Nikola Tesla had also an extreme work culture and even he walked for 13-16 KMS a day. That's insane along with the work.

To create High Energetic Environment, here are a few magical tips that will take your productivity to the extreme in a few days:

- *Always try to wake up near your desk if possible.* I know it's extremely difficult but that's the best way to remind yourself of the tasks you have to accomplish or you can keep significant tasks near you. That would be enough too.

- *Try working in a natural light.* It boosts energy and keeps you energetic for long without hampering your health.

- If you are working in a team, keep your team motivated with a vision. You don't matter to someone until you make them happy. So, break the illusion and become the kindest person they have ever met. Make people comfortable in their true character to bring out their best. The only way to get remembered is when you remember people.

- Steve Jobs often surrounded by people with true potential to do the impossible & believed in them to do the unrealistic but he was rude about the work schedule too.

- *You are the first employee of your work. If you work hard, people will follow your instance.*

- Surround yourself with people of the same vision and energy & thoughts to bring out the same energy. Make sure, you trust yourself and others very well.

- Sometimes we are in a growth stage where our old set of friends don't fit with our vision and we aren't even ready for new ones too. If you friends are the same, I can bet whether you aren't growing or they are growing with or without you.

- ***If you want to be highly obsessed with your goals, don't care too much about people.*** You will piss a lot of people when you want to get surrounded with your goals and make efforts creating an environment where you can work greatly. Marie Curie explained, 'Be less curious about people and more curious about ideas.' Let the world flow with the energy they seek. Don't oppose unless it's necessary.

The greatest education in the world is watching the masters at work. - Michael Jackson.

Nothing great was ever achieved without enthusiasm. - Ralph Waldo Emerson.

The opinion of 10,000 men is of no value if none of them know anything about the subject. - Marcus Aurelius.

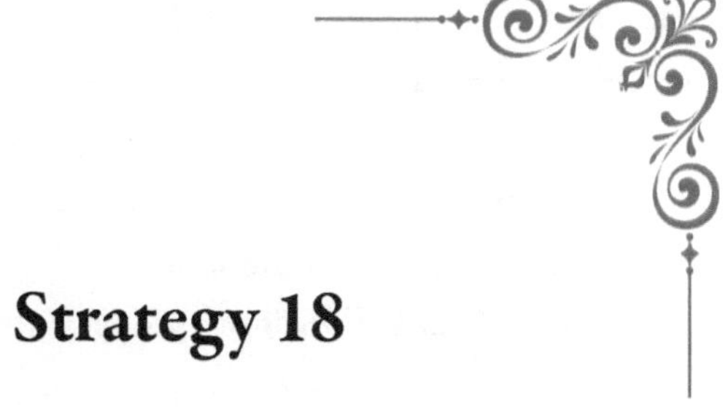

Strategy 18

Mastering the Art of Exceptional Planning for Extraordinary Results: How to Plan Every Little Task in Details & Work on Then Irresistibly!

Purpose of the Strategy: How to plan extraordinarily & work on insane extreme details - Be the extreme details planner – How to split long goals into short term goals & then into daily goals.

If you don't understand the details of your business, you are going to fail. - Jeff Bezos.

A great simplification of every work is damn significant. If you don't understand it well enough in depth, you can't explain it to anyone else. We can't reach perfection but history depicts some people can reach perfection when they do something with deep obsession and that may look like perfection to the audience because it's their own best. There are certain rules that are significant to every person while carrying out their work like Jeff Bezos doesn't take significant decisions after lunch time. I have also imposed some rules on myself to not write when I'm not energetic, feeling lethargic or not hyper active. I write when I feel extraordinarily active with my conscience then I can bring out my best and that can make any work at least close to perfect. Likewise, the nature of goals requires you to go deep because if you leave any stone unturned, you may miss the sense of perfection.

Ancient Greek Philosophers first popularized a concept called ***First Principles Thinking Law which suggests breaking down a complex problem into its most basic and foundational elements to first understand it well by self in simple terms.*** Aristotle believed the best way to understand something is to break it down & then put those parts back together to form a new understanding. That's brilliant. ***Jeff Bezos also uses first principles thinking by resisting proxies at significant events.*** He wants to be in meetings where he should really have. Further, Elon Musk clarified, 'Boil things down to the most fundamental truths & say, OK, what are we sure is true, or as sure as possible is true? And then reason up from there.'

With simplification, you first teach your mind to think clearly and in the same direction. While writing a complex book, first we try to know what values it would generate then boil it down to every little line and word & then a good book is born. Along with long term goals, try split in into short goals and then everyday goals. Split into so small that you don't feel the pressure of achieving the big. You just have to be irresistibly obsessed with your routine and then try proceeding with peace. Don't hurry but enjoy the process!

- We feel, there's a great power in challenging while giving ourselves the impossible tasks while seeking simplicity. If you have a great goal, give yourself the order even if how impossible it is. Just, trust yourself & you will definitely find a way.

- Always begin your day by making yourself happy. That's the first detail. If you are happy then you can make others happy too.

- Anne Frank taught us the great habit of keeping a diary and noting every little detail of what we feel within our soul truly and what we truly seek. She kept her diary to write down her emotions, love, & relationships with her father and herself.

- Plan your every little task in detail by writing everything on a white board, stick some notes, & then making a feasible plan. *Always write down your goals to remember it well.* Plan your next day goals in advance and when the next day comes, you won't have to be stressed about what to do the entire day. Repeat it well. Don't ever plan your day in the morning. You have to plan everything in advance, the last night.

It's the most significant skill, to break down your subject into core elements, then remove what isn't necessary and focus on what matters. Master this skill at any cost because in your everyday life you would find many events that will try consuming your energy but you have to protect yourself well and focus on what truly matter.

Strategy 19

The Manifestation Desk: The True Energy of Law of Attraction & Manifestation!

Purpose of the Strategy: *How self-affirmations are truly underrated - The Power of Surrounding Your Mind with what you want & attracting what you seek!*

I have noticed even people who claim everything is predestined, and that we can do nothing to change it, look before they cross the road. - Stephen Hawking.

Manifestation is logical. We think, what we are trying to seek, we purely seek through a logical experience. A book titled ***'The Secret' by Rhonda Byrne*** is based on such manifestation experiences which depicts, you can get what you want if you imagine it better. Of course, that's true but there's a path. Some people feel the law of attraction works like as we think. What I want a private jet but don't have a car even, then it's a diverse way to disappoint myself soon. ***Whether it's Jim Carry's manifestation to get a $1 Million deal for a mask movie or Shah Rukh Khan to become the king of cinema,***

all manifested with a logical sequence. That's why there's still some ongoing debates on whether manifestation really works or not. So, if I think I'm immortal then It's purely an act of foolishness. It's out of possibility. Likewise, there's always some possibility of what we are doing. Irresistible Obsession book focus on sequence wise methods that tell you to focus on what you do and you can break any mountain in half.

Nikola Tesla created a 365-manifestation method which worked for him very well. We feel if you seek something, you have to be irresistibly mad about it so you can prepare that required potential during the journey. That's the trick. If I want to be a good writer, then I have to think about it all again and again and again until I start doing hard work and making efforts for it. So, manifestation isn't magic but it tricks your brain to make you feel like you can do it even if you can't until you become the person who can. Logically, it's marvellous & magical but it includes hard work to prepare ourselves for what we are seeking. *According to the 369-manifestation method, we should write down our desired manifestation clearly and remember it well in our minds. Here, 3 represents writing down manifestation 3 times in the morning and 6 times during the day and 9 times in the evening. We have to do this for 21 or more days to make it our habit.* This looks stupid but once your mind remembers it, it will guide you well in the right direction. Also, Nikola Tesla died all alone and in debt at a cheap hotel in New York City but for his goals of inventions, he succeeded very well. *Tesla's 369 theory mentioned 3,6,9 numbers are the keys to understanding the universe. These numbers exist as energy without losing their identity.*

Another manifestation technique we found is Creative Visualization, a cognitive process that involves creating mental images either with eyes open or closed. It depicts the power of focusing on one like meditation, imagination, thoughts and ultimately manifestation. Also, it advises us to see ourselves where we want to see, like on the stage getting awards for doing the best work in our field or having a lot of money, wealth & success or see what we really want to become honestly.

Also, there's an **80/20 Rule**, known as ***Parito Principle which clarifies that 80% of the output of results will come from 20% of the inputs or action.*** So, we have to keep going to increase the probability of our success by overcoming what we want. This is the logical way to see ourselves where we actually want to.

- Follow your gut feeling as it forms subconsciously after the events & patterns. It's basically your instinct and energy that form with dots, patterns and actions.

- Put this in your mind, you will always win when you really want to. When you feel like you can win, you will surely. That's the true manifestation. You have to make it visible instead of working on it silently. There's no scope for failure until you want to.

- Your attitude is your destiny, not the situations. History reveals, people who once told about the impossibility of something, they made it happen and that reflects how much your obsession & passion are significant. Your attitude is your destiny.

- ***Ralph Waldo Emerson voiced, 'Once you make a decision, the universe conspires to make it happen.'***

If you think all the time: "I am a genius." You will eventually become a genius. - Salvador Dali.

Strategy 20

The Brilliance of Strategic Inaction: How to Do Nothing & Stay Idle for The Best Ideas

Purpose of the Strategy: *The real power of doing nothing - The Art of staying idle - The art of idleness to create more energy than being consumed.*

Only simplicity can solve complexity.

Pablo Picasso suggested, without great solitude, no serious work is possible. The best work doesn't exist only when we are obsessed with our work but during the entire time. I often ask people what they do when they have nothing to do. What we actually do when we are idle because that's also the great source of energy. In most of the chapters we suggested attacking the work as soon as you wake up but history reveals diversions when it comes to passionate work. Some world best personalities like *William Shakespeare woke up at 4am and wrote the world's best literature and on the other side, there's*

133

            DEEPAK GUPTA

Pablo Picasso who woke up at 11'o clock in the morning and made himself the most obsessed and productive artist ever. It's damn true, our most energy get utilized in what we don't love because at the same time we are doing and resisting it and that's tremendously double utilization of energy while on the other side when we really want to do some work, we follow the direction and spend less energy and go for too long but it's damn true, it's not every time that we would only get the work we love. Some day we also have to do the most hated work but, in that process, we get consumed for too long. We lose too much of our energy and here comes the need of understanding the art of being alone; the real power of how to do nothing while doing something and save our energy. Idleness is an art and if we get idle with the right things, we may get more energy for the work we truly love.

We feel, we shouldn't oppose what we don't love it from our heart because sometimes situations force us to do these hated works but you can save your peace and energy while not opposing it. Idleness is necessary for creating energy so we can focus on our work later but some people get more consumed in the idleness and don't reach their loving work with reasonable energy. *I accomplish my writing in three phases of two hours each including a 30-minute break in every session.* After two hours of intense work, I didn't get much tired but I observed myself, I got indulged in some activities, like talking to people & got more consumed in between and as expected, didn't reach the third cycle. That half hour of Idleness should prepare me for the next session so, if my Idleness is consuming my more energy, then what's the point of doing nothing or taking rest in between. That nothing is consuming me more than when I really do something and that's horrible. Also, I observed, after we do our most loving work, we release more positive energy and we really have to save it but most people make such mistakes of getting indulged in wrong work and waste their energy in happiness. Never waste your energy even if you are glad after doing your work. ***Stay energetic.***

- Even our hobbies, past time, idleness, & void should be of our interest, so we don't ever get drain in our lives. ***Charlie Chaplin loved to play the violin in his idle time while Bill Gates loved to read newspapers & books.*** We have observed, the greatest personalities of all time were focused and cared for what they actually had to do in their idle time. Even Nikola Tesla loved to walk more than 10 miles for mind refreshment but now a day, we are consumed more with the internet, overthinking, lots of irrelevant problems and nothing. *Remember, the great personalities & artists remain calm & occupied with what doesn't drain them.*

- If you are doing something in your idle time, don't oppose, just go with the flow to protect your energy and mind from getting exhausted.

- Even accomplish the irrelevant work like play, so you can take your energy to the long way to accomplish the significant tasks of the day.

- ***It's true, you have to keep doing your worst to reach better & then you can reach your best.***

- Art is the best form to remain idle. You can paint, write, or follow a nature trail where you can feel peaceful while doing it. It shouldn't be your primary obsession but something that prepares you for the primary obsession. Remember, don't spend your energy even if you want to do nothing because that would make you feel insane & tired when you want to accomplish your loving work.

- Steve Jobs really had a simple life and we often ask ourselves, why these rich people don't live their lives in the big & bright lime lights while throwing out money on their paths. I have a great answer; because when you are happy with what you are doing, even the diamonds feel dull in front of them and that's simple proof, we don't want the best but what we really seek. ***Steve Jobs once mentioned, 'I have a simple life. I have my family & I have Apple & Pixar.' Haha.***

- Don't give too much space to things that require much energy. Remove what drains you continuously and do it ruthlessly. Grow energy and compound it every day. Focus on every atom and detail and you will fly. The world inside you would become so beautiful even in the worst of chaos too.

- It's accepted, you feel lonely when you are less intelligent and less focused on your goals. Only boring people get bored. If you can't entertain yourself, you can't entertain anyone. We all can live alone with more happiness even in the state of idleness but it happens when we feel true happiness in what we honestly love.

- ***Take deep rest & then focus on your work deeply.*** By doing more work while tiring ourselves, we destroy our focus and remain more idle too. The great focus lies on how we reach towards the work while utilizing our idleness in the right way without getting exhausted. Always keep your habit of taking rest. It's the best pleasure when we take a rest after doing the most loving work of our lives.

This life is what you make it. No matter what, you're going to mess up sometimes, it's a universal truth. But the

good part is you get to decide how you're going to mess it up. -
Marilyn Monroe.

Strategy 21

The Telltale Signs of True Obsession with Your Passion!

No matter what you do, give it everything you have. Be the best, not the second best. - Michael Jackson.

Zack stated, 'When you are truly obsessed with your Passion, you don't force yourself to work but force yourself to stop.' When you love something more than anything else in this world, every problem would vanish in front of it and you can tackle even the worst failures in that loving work. The matter is, how significant it's for your soul and nothing else. The more you start something out of reasons, the more you will stop yourself in the process in the absence of those reasons. If you want to succeed in something, you can't reach your best because you started a goal with a reason and you will stop as soon as you get it. There shouldn't be any reason but only love that you would even choose that work on your last day but funny thing is, after everything, all will be forgotten. You don't know how much obsessed you are until you get failed or succeed as much as the mortal world wants. *The intensity ends when we begin with a reason. For constant, rising and compounding fire, you have to choose your passion without any reason; just your passion that even if you get nothing or no success with it, there would be no relevant effect.* Humans don't reach their greatness because they stop themselves often and feel they are successful enough. The only failure is when we feel we are successful enough now.

In the entire book Irresistible Obsession, we focus on being obsessed with your passion, so you can become your best, not someone else's best and we have found some signs that may take you to your best and assist you to know whether you are going ahead or not:

- A truly passionate person is never attracted towards success or failure because after anything, he may stop with that accomplishment or reason. The key to your best is to feel unsatisfied with your best or take inspiration from your best to reach the perfection. You shouldn't be attracted to success or failure and not even get affected.

- Once Alexander the Great cried when he realised there were more worlds out there and he declared in sadness, *'There were more worlds out there and I haven't even conquered one.'* To perceive this positively, he knew how much potential he had to shake the entire world with his obsession. Even if you don't appreciate & value the world's best, it will remain the best. No matter.

- Another sign, you can be wonderful and influential with your fire. Nikola Tesla was the most wonderful and influential people in the world because his main invention Alternative Current motor powers the entire world until now. Success isn't everything but only our love towards the work because in that love, we live every atom well.

- ***Risk is an extremely stupid fear in this world but it changes its position as soon as we overcome it.*** When a child is afraid to cross the road, a man assists him in overcoming his fear. If you want to overcome any fear, defeat it by trying or winning over it. Most people regret at the end of their lives when realise, they were enough capable to change the world but even forgot to change themselves. Your fear would be high if today's the first day of your life, but if it's the last day, fear is stupid. Every day is the last day. Kick fear in the teeth, right to break its jaw. Never say no to the risk, that's the biggest risk.

- ***A true obsessed one isn't afraid to carry out the impossible.*** There's always one who overcomes the impossible with his passion because passion breaks every barrier. We get to know; Elon Musk uses the first principle of thinking that says to read people's minds to know & analyse what they really need. What their true future needs. Ultimately, he wishes to fulfil the impossible to go to the mars one day because he wants to.

- ***A true passionate person undertakes his work every day, no matter what.*** Even if the sky is falling, he would do it. It's a misconception that you have to force yourself to work, No, you have to stop yourself from work you love. You will do it every day, no matter what. You will dance with it like Vincent Van Gogh, Michael Jackson or Pablo Picasso.

- Another sign is, after doing your loving work, you will feel energetic, not consumed because good work creates more energy and that energy should be directed to work more and then it's the best loop to stay in it. While worst is, if you force yourself to work, you would get consumed and then exhausted later and after that in pressure, more exhausted and finally a worst loop to make you tired for life. In a great work of your soul, you feel energetic, not consumed. Also, you will create and feel energetic while doing it.

- *Alexander the Great taught me, a leader is always in the front.* He led & fought all his fights from the front even in the critical battles. You lead by example, not by saying and learn most when you are in the front otherwise what's the use of a true leader if he's not skilful enough to lead.

- *I bet, you can't live alone for more than two days but a true passionate can do it easily* because when most people are alone, they can't entertain themselves for long. They try enough to entertain themselves while true artists do that fluently because they don't even try to. They just feel lost in his work and would never know whether they were alone or lonely. Writing teaches me the great art of solitude, to stay alone in the right way to bring out the best in my soul. Trust me, you can live alone and even with great happiness and feel lose into your own soul.

- A more focused a person is, a more loving work he's doing. You will have great focus when you want to do some work. Also, focus is not something to put pressure on yourself but it comes automatically when you do your work honestly. You will forget everything. People who focus on being focused aren't actually focused.

- Another sign of being truly obsessed; problems are nothing for you. Every problem is invisible and you don't have to be hampered by them. Problems become distractions when you are doing something against your will and then every little problem would look big for you. *Only undertake the most passionate work and you don't need to change anything.* You will do it even if someone shoots you in your chest. I'm sorry, I don't have a better instance than this. You have to see your goals big enough and problems small. When goals are big and significant, every big problem is just a peanut.

- I feel, passionate people don't find pleasure in other tasks to divert their minds. They just feel best when they do their work. The best instance is, Shah Rukh Khan.

- Even if the entire world is on fire, you should remain calm with your skills, obsession, work and confidence. Of course, you will do it even on the last day of your life.

I would rather die of passion than of boredom. - Vincent Van Gogh - Damn he voiced the entire life is a line.

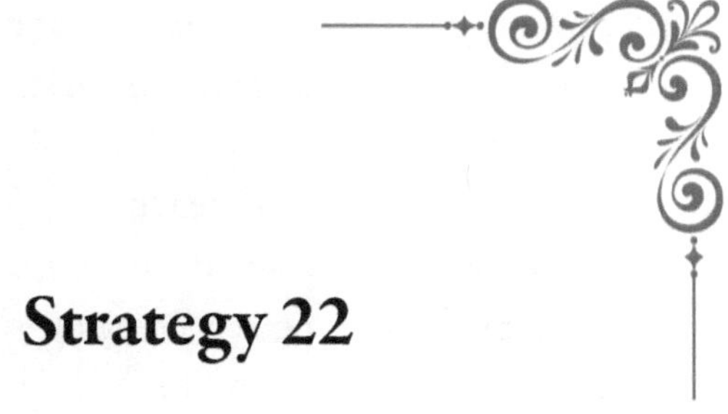

Strategy 22

Only Boring People Get Bored: Why Intense Passionate People Love to Stay Alone - How to Be Alone Without Ever Feeling Lonely

Purpose of the Strategy: The power of staying alone - why artists are afraid of humans & how they get lost into another dimension so flawlessly!

It's not that I'm so smart. It's just that I stay with problems longer. - Albert Einstein.

When was the last time you sit alone with yourself without doing anything? You know, people feel afraid of being alone because that forces them to face the reality of their lives and own souls. It's very arduous for evil souls to face themselves because once they realise, they are doing wrong deeds, they would die of their own guilt. We keep avoiding the truth of life until we face the last day of our lives. It's better to live a life where you already know the bitter truth than avoiding it again & again. I have done deep research on many artists and found, most were gloomy & passionate but enlightened. Of course, life makes us feel negative because it was designed like this and that's why we have to be super conscious to do good deeds. Every loner feels like a disgrace to society but they aren't. On one side when most people are afraid of being alone, there are some intense passionate people who beg for self-care and alone time to analyse themselves and the entire world to accomplish their goals. It's the simplicity that can solve complexity. When we really sit with ourselves, we find the absolute truth. Because without solitude, there's no possibility of the best work. If you are a creative person or an artist, you try creating a new world where you are already interacting with energies that make you feel fulfilled and not bored. I found, most people do something else for their work and beg for other people's attention because they don't get fulfilled by their own work. So, they have to chase something else to get fulfilled while artists are already fulfilling themselves with their work and love to stay alone and even reject social interaction if it consumes them. A creative person doesn't get bored easily and doesn't even seek much social interaction.

In life, you will realise most problems or situations arise out of human relationships but artists don't want to destroy their peace after indulging in them.

- When artists are alone, they try seeing the clear picture while involving every atom and bringing out the best details. Vincent Van Gogh created Starry Night in a mental asylum all alone even if his mental condition wasn't that good. To create masterpieces, artists need alone time and sometimes that wouldn't be enough. I felt when Nikola Tesla voiced, 'I need solitude for my writing, not like a hermit, that wouldn't be enough but like a dead man.' He often wrote most of his books during the entire night. We know, we had already mentioned his quote in some previous chapter too. It's a gentle reminder.

- The vast sea has immense salt but without tasting its own depth & intensity, it would never know. Likewise, when we go outside in this world, we absorb every good and bad but it wouldn't come out until we think of it cautiously. I'm amazed when we go inside our own soul, there's no way anyone can disturb us.

- Most artists love to be around strangers, so they can get to know those people without even getting noticed.

- ***If you want to be a loner, you have to learn your own character and know what you really love.*** Meanwhile, you can always choose a good book, soothing music, having a nice pet, getting obsessed with your work and living with acceptance. Don't ever skip a task you really love. Don't regret & live happily in your own state. Nothing will really matter after a certain period of time.

- For good loners, intelligent and creative people, human interaction is a curse. To go inside, you have to free yourself from the outside world of what people really think about you. You have to choose your own space where you can explore the caves of your mysterious soul.

- You know, if you are afraid of being alone, you can't be creative & knowing yourself correctly. Sit down with yourself.

- ***People are poison for artists.*** They aren't distracted with people but actually highly obsessed with what they do so they want to love it every moment.

- ***Stephen Hawking*** suggested us to explain everything in simple terms so that everyone can understand. His most famous book, ***A Brief History of Time, sold more than 10 million copies which depicts his amazing genius mind, incredible deep determination, simplicity of explanation, curiosity & discipline.***

Intelligent people can live alone. They know how to occupy themselves intelligently without human interaction or wasteful activities.

Quiet people have the loudest minds. - Stephen Hawking.

Strategy 23

Build Legitimate High Resilience for Failure: Trick Your Mind - The Purpose of Failure in Personal & Professional Growth!

Purpose of the Strategy: *How to free from fear of urging more - Choose your soul & loving work - Do we have the scope of failure? Failure has a strong purpose!*

I have missed more than 9,000 shots in my career. I have lost almost 300 games. On 26 occasions I have been entrusted to take the game winning shot, and I missed. I have failed over & over & over again in my life. And that's why I succeeded. - Michael Jordan.

What does a man gain from his failure? Ultimately, A great strong skill, bravery and unbeatable resilience. History has mentioned the most successful people who got terribly failed in the same career in which they got succeed massively. No one even gave a penny to Vincent Van Gogh & he ended up with depression and miserable death in poverty but now his paintings are fetching billions. He once spoke, *'Success is sometimes the outcome of a whole string of failures.'* We feel every failure has a purpose to make us better and then best because humans have the habits to exaggerate their own intensity of success when it comes to them easily. The time you live with failure isn't wasted. You earn bravery with that. I have been writing for more than 8 years and I know I have improved a lot while finding my own mistakes and embracing my failures. In the worst case, trick your mind to see failure as your teacher. Buddha said, what you think you become because if you can think it, you can also build the capabilities by learning to achieve that but think if people aren't even thinking about their capabilities then how they can build them. Hence, first, every masterpiece form in our minds and then in reality. ***Trust me, those who get afraid of failure, really get failed.*** Also, failure is a pure illusion because our success can be a failure to someone too, so, we all have to set our own standards in which we want to succeed.

Now, how anyone can trick his mind. Here we have mentioned some instances to make you feel how much significant it is to be failed:

- Vincent Van Gogh failed in his entire life. That's terrible but now he's the best post-impressionist painter in the entire history but before he died, he even realised a lot that he was best.

- Even the world's best writers got terribly rejected in the beginning. Stephen King novel Carrie got rejected 30 times by publishers and even J.K. Rowling's Harry Potter got rejected by many publishers. Everyone has a story to tell. The stairs of perfection start with failure. Trick your mind that it's just a phase of learning. You fail, learn and go ahead & trust me perfection is waiting for you at the top.

- Before you take one shot of success, live 1,000 shots of failure. Your success is only one step ahead. Failures help us learning the skills to shake the world. Be hopeful and start working.

- J.K. Rowling sounded, 'Feel like you have nothing to lose & you can do your best, fearlessly & endlessly.'

- After deep research, we found, people who were failing deeply in their specific fields, they later became the world's best in those skills because they created an intense fire in their hearts. There's something really planned by God. If we don't get terribly failed, we don't become conscious of ourselves. Your failures aren't wasted. If even after your best efforts, you get failed, God is preparing you for world class success.

- Failure brings you closer to success. *Thomas Edison proclaimed, 'Many of life's failures were people who did not realise how close they were to success when they gave up.'*

- Always remember, success can come to us at any point of time. Just keep working honestly.

- Some people wait for the problems or mess to get end so they can finish what matters to them. The distractions, lessons, problems, and mistakes would never leave you. Let's finish the best work in between the mess. There's no right time to do the best work.

- Isaac Newton depicted, 'My powers are ordinary. Only my application brings me success.'

- Luck & fear both are stupid. Only people who try enough times get succeed and make their own luck.

- Success and failures have diverse meanings and dimensions. For some people walking is a dream while for some running is a dream. Our success depends on how satisfied we are, until then we should keep trying for what we really love.

What would life be if we had no courage to attempt anything. - Vincent Van Gogh.

Do it big, do it right and do it with style. - Fred Astaire.

Success is a failure in progress. - Albert Einstein.

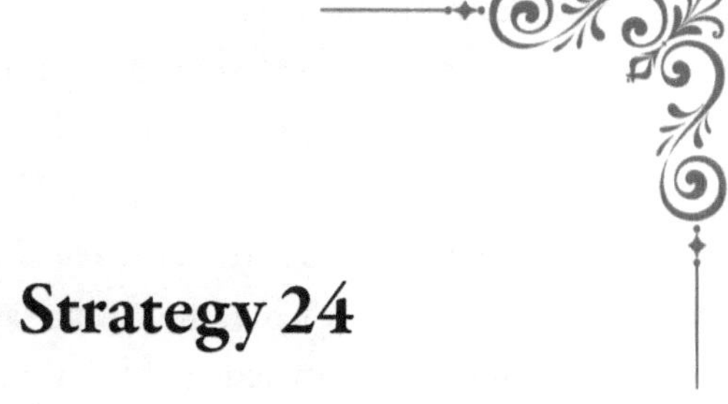

Strategy 24

Self-Teaching Skills - How Self-Directed Learning Transformed My Life - How Do You Really Think About Yourself!

A great writer is mostly found between the words.

If everything is planned then why we are here and what's the logic of karma, good or evil if we were already forced to do what was destined but trust me, it was never like that. Now, what I'm writing ahead would astonish you for so long. *Every world class genius is self-taught.* They mostly told themselves they wanted to be, so best that they can't be replaced. Put differently, or they just became themselves so when people try their best, they can't be because every person has some unique traits that made him tremendous and skilful. That's why we suggest you to find your lovable work because that's a play and when in the beginning you love the play, then you would go intense to make it best. We don't want our lovable thing to be normal. William Shakespeare, one of the world's best literary figures, never attended any university. We all get pushed into the situations but we always have a choice to seek what we truly love. It's damn true, those who are satisfied in being mediocre, remain mediocre because they accept their destiny. There's nothing like destiny in this world. It's just the human perspective to make themselves satisfied.

Michael Jordan was a self-trained dancer. He never went training or to school for dancing, that says how much he was interested when he really learned by himself. In self Teaching, you get the freedom to do what you want and in what intensity. You can go beyond anything because it would matter to you.

Even ***Vincent Van Gogh was also a self-taught painter.*** He's the perfect instance of continue doing what you really love. When you love something, you become irresistible even without results and then you try to make it good, better, best and perfect. You just do it for yourself because you feel so good while doing it while others may wonder why you are becoming so obsessed with it. We feel, once we know what we love, we should teach ourselves a lot because that brings up the real consciousness and awareness to beat ourselves again and again. You know, in the last two months of his life, Vincent Van Gogh entered into one of his most energetic & creative periods, completing one painting per day. Also, when Vincent believed in himself, he felt it was necessary to master black and white before attempting to work in colour. That's damn impressive when you find your way instead of asking from people who know nothing about your passion. Unfortunately, he wasn't widely recognised during his lifetime.

Self-Teaching has been changing my life a lot and I'm becoming the person I want to be. Once I was searching for a lot of techniques on how a book gets published and year after years, I have learned a lot by solving the relevant problems.

Every problem has also a question & that should be answered to get more relevant problems.

Elon Musk depicted, 'I think it's possible for ordinary people to choose extraordinary.' He added, 'When something is important enough, you do it even if the odds are not in your favour. It's insane that Elon Musk works like a mad man, at least 100 hours a week. We all choose our intensity, love and obsession. An interested person was never forced. ***Do you think Pablo Picasso was told to make more than 1.5 lakh paintings?*** We all are employed in the wrong areas because this bullshit society pushes us well into fixed areas instead of asking what we truly want.

Self-Teaching can be done in many ways:

- ***Always try finishing what you started. Make it a habit.*** Make this your classical conditioning. Finish gracefully what you started with. Don't leave until you are done.

- Always solve relevant problems than solving every problem. Good problems are always fun to solve.

- Don't bother about fear for a second when you're learning something. Go insane for what you love, otherwise there are a lot of sane people blaming fear and other situations.

- If you love something and don't own any skills, you have to learn them for a long time but one day you will be skilful and successful. Skills are the key in the 21st century. As jobs are vanishing, upgrade your skills. You have every right to upgrade yourself to become superhuman.

- Remember, time is the most valuable skill in teaching. If you don't invest time, you don't deserve perfection.

- ***Alexander the Great had Aristotle as his teacher but he was immensely self-taught.*** It's a rumour or not but no one in this world had palms like Alexander in this world. He had a mystic cross between his head and heart line in both palms and he even followed his palmistry seriously and it's laughable that he even checked the palms of most soldiers in his kingdom to know what they truly were in their destiny. That's purely a matter of debate.

- Remember, in obsession, you would mostly have less time or feel you are short of it because sometimes other people would also demand more time from you; maybe you love yourself. Protect your time and be ruthless if you have to. That's the rule.

- ***Education is significant but learning practical skills is more significant than education.*** History clarifies, it's not the most educated that become genius but the super conscious mind minds. So, sharpen your mind and focus because your capabilities and right work are enough. When you love something from the depths of your heart, it's enough. That's it. You will always find a way.

- In this society, your awareness and values beat intelligence. When people asked, what should be the qualities of a genius? I laughed and elaborated, he may or may not be super intelligent or most educated but should be fearless, curious, strong, risk taker and kind. ***When Alexander the Great was asked, 'Who shall have the empire' & he replied, 'to the strongest.'*** Meanwhile he could also suggest to give the entire kingdom to the intelligent but he knew, intelligence isn't the trait to become the world's strongest. This world has enough intelligent people. Damn.

- *The founder of Adidas, Adolf Dassler taught us, 'Be creative, work independently and take action & responsibility for your work.*' He voiced, 'Quality brought Adidas to the top & only quality guarantees our success.' He added, 'Test, test and test again.'

- Don't ever feel like you are an alien if your interests are extremely different from society's opinions. You are unique if you are too different. Sometimes we call such thinking as alienation. Under this, there are some people who often perceive themselves or others to be outsiders or social misfits. They don't get easily fit in society norms and feel unwelcomed in certain areas of society. Due to such alienation, at the time of Franz Kafka's death, he instructed his friend Brod to burn all his manuscripts including all his letters and diaries but now everyone is reading and appreciating him while he doubted himself the entire time. Even *Adolf Hitler once was a painter but got rejected for his admission in the art school and he even doubted himself because he wanted justification for his arts.* It's good to doubt ourselves but the right confidence is extremely needed to train ourselves in the right form.

- *Before you teach a lot to others, first teach yourself. Become what you pretend to be.*

Intelligence keeps you ahead. Smartness takes you far.

Life doesn't forgive fearless. - Adolf Hitler.

Strategy 25

Shift Your Position of Motivation – How Money Can Never Be the End Goal for True Obsessed Artists

I am not interested in money. I just want to be wonderful.
- Merilyn Monroe.

You need a lot of money to say money doesn't matter but have you ever wondered, history has the list of world's best geniuses who had immense wealth and prosperity but they weren't very much fascinated by them. A great work starts with love and stays with it forever. It irresistibly increases with time but never ends. If something starts with some kind of motivation, then it would may end with the fulfilment of that motivation. To be irresistibly obsessed with your work, you shouldn't work with motivation or any kind of external factors. After observing the wealthy personalities, most people make such mistakes to copy them & choose their work for money and that's the biggest mistake anyone can do with their lives. If I take deep interest in paintings, then it doesn't mean I can be a painter. I also have to know my interest & capabilities honestly. Really, I have to choose something that would be with me for a lifetime without any motivation or money but the bitter truth is people choose money over themselves and their motivation ends with time when they realise, they were never after the money or anything else. That's bitter. Money is the best and worst motivation of all time. Money takes you far but some day you will definitely stop if you are after money. Money can bring freedom for life but can't provide the self-accomplishment we seek every moment.

- ***Nikola Tesla got failed in financial matters*** so terribly that he died in a hotel, penniless and in poverty. Vincent Van Gogh shot himself in the wheat field and he also died penniless. But both were marvellous in their fields and you know, because of their poverty they don't know what they value they provided to the society. Be valuable instead of running towards money or other factors as motivation.

- Passionate people sometimes fail in financial matters because we all know, we also have to work for our livelihood. Artistic work looks good when you have enough money. That's why it's difficult to shift your point of motivation. If it was easy, everyone would come and make it crowded. If you have found the meaning of your life, live it well. Most people don't know what they are really doing.

- ***To do the greatest work of all time, you don't need motivation but have to be yourself and then go insane for your love.*** Money was never the end goal otherwise the great would never become greatest. It's something inside us that prepares for perfection, self-accomplishment, magic, madness, & create a fire inside our hearts. The greatest people have the brightest & longest fire in their hearts. Money is the worst motivation of all time. Find yourself and everything will fall into place. The way is different.

- Okay, we all need money too. I hope you aren't unhappy with what I said about money but for passionate people, it's true wealth. They don't run towards money but time. Time is the entire wealth and if you can utilise it well along with your passion, you become unbeatable. To get unlimited money, you have to distract yourself from money & follow your passion because at the end you have to taste your satisfaction along with money too. If seeking money is the worst motivation of all time then enough money is also.

- Don't ever waste too much time motivating yourself. All days aren't equal. Get inspired by your own work while following your passion.

- To start something for your soul, you have to find yourself! Find things beautiful and you will find what matters to you. We have to find our love, not motivation or any factor that arouses us for a limited time.

- Cassius says in Julius Caesar, 'Men at some time are masters of their fates: the fault, dear Brutus, is not in our stars, but in ourselves, that we are underlings.' Pure. Pure.

- Choose your love and you won't ever have to find motivation for your work. Motivation is void.

Most people try bringing out more from their life after money but they should focus more on bringing out what they want before the greediness of money or pleasure.

Find things beautiful as much as you can, most people find too little beautiful. - Vincent Van Gogh.

Strategy 26

The Unrecognized Artists of History: Extracting Knowledge & Skills from The World's Leading Artists - Why They Were Never Failed in Life!

Purpose of the Strategy: Learning from the world's best artists even they failed in their lives with money and fame & finally, what they can teach us to become an irresistible artist!

People discuss my art and pretend to understand it as if it were necessary to understand, when it's simply necessary to love. - Claude Monet.

History remembers the artists but there also comes a time in the artist's phase when no one remembers them in any place. If you are unique, most people see it as diversity and alienation to society. To be with society, you have to follow the norms but artists have no boundaries. They work in free verse but to earn money and fame, they should also be accepted by a wide society as well. Hence, it's a damn challenge to please society and as well as to create something that they love too. *Pablo Picasso voiced, 'A great artist doesn't sell what people want to buy but sells what he creates.'* If you have to adjust yourself according to people, then you can't be honest with yourself and your art.

For an artist, success and failures are subjective. Some artists are happy with not getting fame or enough money while some feel if they don't get fame, they aren't as successful as they want to be. That's why some people avoid being creative because creativity is extremely risky when it comes to earning your livelihood through it. You have to make a bridge between what you love and what people want! When ***Claude Monet depicted, 'Nothing in the whole world is of interest to me but my painting and my flowers,'*** I really felt that. For an artist, the honest work is his true success. If he can continue working, he's successful because he's creating what he loves. So, instead of thinking about failed artists & calling them failed, think about artists who were much ahead of their time and not widely accepted in society. If you scrounge articles and research, you will find many artists who weren't well known in their time but after their death, they become the most successful artists in the world and the most significant skill we can learn from unrecognized artists is, they continued their work! Out honest suggestion, continue doing what you truly love. Also, history remarked, there were a lot of artists who even destroyed their own work because they doubted themselves too much. It's damn true, an artist mostly seeks appreciation from people who understand their art.

We have found a small list of unrecognized artists and clarified what we can learn from them:

- In our list, ***Vincent Van Gogh*** is on the top always because he started his post-impressionist painting career very late and ended abruptly. He was penniless and even borrowed money from his brother Theo for buying canvas and paints. We found a few attributes in him. He never stopped his work even when his mental condition wasn't good. In the asylum he created the stunning historical Starry Night painting. ***Whether we call this madness or not, a genius artist is always an obsessed person above every sane activity.***

- *Claude Monet sounded, 'I had so much fire in me & so many plans.'* It's true when you find the purpose of your life and find something that truly fascinates you and even you have the power of control to make yourself happy, you become mad even if no one likes it. Claude Monet's most paintings looked incomplete & ugly that he received a lot of hate from the entire world. In that context, he wrote, 'My life has been nothing but a failure.' It's true, these artists seek the best from their lives that they find themselves too weak. Their dream to seek more & more, made them realise how little they know about themselves. They go mad but still feel unsatisfied, maybe finding the core.

- Another unrecognized personality was an ***American Poet, Emily Dickinson who only published 10 poems in his lifetime but after her death, her sister found 1,800 poems which made her the most renowned poet in history. I really loved her line, 'Forever is composed of nows.'***

- It's interesting to know, most artists were unrecognized and seemed to have failed but they were truly alive in their hearts & that's what is significant. Instead of asking for success, you should know how to be truly alive & happy with yourself. I think that's the most significant yet ignorable part of our society.

- Do you remember the famous painting of the girl with pearl earrings? Affirmative, it was made by world famous Dutch painter of all time, ***Johannes Vermeer***. He was irresistibly famous for intimate household scenes paintings with astounding light. Unfortunately, he also died of short illness, leaving his wife & children in poverty but now his paintings are also fetching billions. We have learned, in between the failure, if you are doing the most significant lovable thing, you don't have to motivate yourself but the interesting thing is, when you do what you love, you don't need motivation. You will dance on the fire of your work. That's significant & powerful. ***The cost of being an artist is his own life. With limited genius arts of the dead artists, their art begins to rise and value peaks in their absence.***

*- **Have you seen the movie, The Pursuit of Happiness?*** I will not give you a spoiler but the idea of a main character, ***Chris Gardener*** who told the most vital feelings of every passionate person, ***'Don't ever let someone tell you that you can't do something. Not even me. You got a dream, you got to protect it. When people can't do something themselves, they're going to tell you that you can't do it. You want something, go get it. Period.'***

- Creating what you love is truly a successful life. If you are creating the work even in your failure, you're not ordinary, my friend. Also, great arts are created slowly, very slowly that you absorb the details and make every atom visible to everyone. You put every emotion into the work along with your sweat. When you take most interest in that thing, you treat it as extraordinary. You don't skip it even if you are exhausted. You make it brilliant bit by bit and finally a true masterpiece gets ready.

- A right insanity is the dough of an artist. Edgar Allan Poe put into words, 'I do not suffer from insanity, I enjoy every minute of it.'

- If you want to learn from the world's best, read the books written by people who had overcome their problems forever. Isaac Newton depicted, 'If I have seen further it is by standing on the shoulders of Giants.'

- Many people don't know the world's famous poet, *John Keats died at the age of only 25 years due to Tuberculosis.* It's a pleasure for our hearts to feel; 'A thing of beauty is a joy forever. Its loveliness increases; it will never pass into nothingness.'

'There's no plan B for Passion.' - Chris Gardener. And he also mentioned, 'It's okay to fail; it's not okay to quit.'

An artist cannot fail; it is a success to be one. - Charles Horton Cooley.

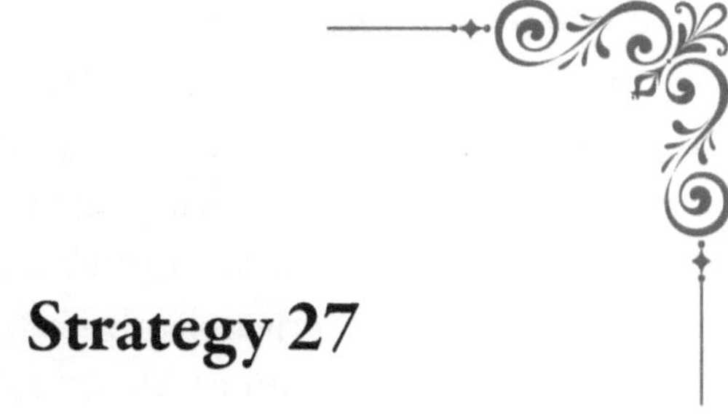

<h1 style="text-align:center">Strategy 27</h1>

The Golden Ancient Life Principles, Philosophies & Hidden Unexplored Techniques That Are Missing in Our Generation to Create Artistic Life - Embracing the Passion: History of The Most Passionate People of The Universe

Purpose of the Strategy: What was so special in the ancient times that people were so talented, genius & great artists. Exploring the in-depth philosophies of some great personalities. What still makes us wonder. What qualities did they have?

With discipline you can beat the most talented people but with obsession, you can win yourself which is far better than winning the entire world.

How to be passionate? I usually ask myself the same question again & again so, I can live every day like a dream moment, where I can attain peace without seeking it. We already mentioned, every work is a work of art and if you feel like you are making art, you can make it irresistibly interesting and soulful. What actually matter for an artistic life! What was so special in ancient times that people were so creative and innovative! After analysing the world's best passionate people, we have created a set of principles that can make anyone a great artist with their implantation! These are the real qualities of people who were damn more peaceful and passionate than the people of our generation!

- ***Michelangelo Buonarroti*** shared, '***The greatest danger for most of us is not that our aim is too high and we miss it, but that it is too low and we reach it.***' It's purely a betrayal to lives when we seek only little dreams and suppress our big dreams because we build the void fear of being failed in their hearts. I read somewhere, 'The more fearful the person is the more he would use his mind. The less fearful the person is the more he would use his heart.' Even the most intelligent people calculate too much and suppress themselves for living their dream life. ***Until an intelligent person thinks, a fool accomplishes masterpieces with his hard work.*** That's the difference. Our ancient personalities were more inclined to curiosity than to feel fear. Always aim too high even if you fail because failure is nothing but an illusion just like success. You have to love your soul and that's it. Now, never ever criticize the man who is doing his work honestly and becoming happy in what he does.

- Our ancestors had a great attribute of being patient to accomplish anything. Even if you find a sculpture, gardner or painter, they all were extremely patient with their process. If you hurry in the process, you don't learn the real details of an art. *Michelangelo Buonarroti sounded, 'Genius is eternal peace.'* We feel, atom by atom, a great world is created that has so many flowers to discover just like the creations of god. Build the high level of patience and you will learn more than you seek.

- *I feel, neither it's the talent that wins in the end nor the genius but the man with courage and will. Talent is an illusion.* Practice can take us to beyond everything. When you practice a lot with what you love, you will become obsessed. What's better than being super skilled in the work you truly worship. Michelangelo Buonarroti was an Italian sculptor &, painter and he also died penniless but he clarified, 'It is well with me when I have a chisel in my hand.' *Also, Edward Munch depicted, 'My will exceeds my talents.'*

- Now, this will astonish you for too long. *Life is purely negative and gloomy. It was designed like that.* It's the true nature of life and it's easy to flow with it. If every tree is giving us shade, then it's their nature. River flows, sun rises and sets, and that's their nature. Hence, I have learned, life is purely negative and sad because it's extremely easy to be negative in life without much efforts but if you want to be happy and peaceful, you have to make conscious efforts and even if you lose it for a moment, you may lose that consciousness & fall into the gulf of sadness again. So, we should learn about being super conscious, so we can live well. In that context, Edward Munch stated, 'What is art? Art grows from joy and sorrow, but mostly from sorrow. It grows from human lives.'

- *Another genius rule; if you want to live extremely well, open your heart than mind.* The truth of life is in the softness of the heart where you give love and learn extremely well. Love makes you humble. From ancient times, every artist was focused on love because it's damn true. If you want to live well, leave your focus from winning to loving. Even with less, you will live well. Edward Munch voiced some brilliant words, 'I don't believe in an art that is not born out of man's need to open his heart.'

- I found the greatest artists of all time were in absolute solitude whether it was Franz Kafka, Anne Frank, Vincent Van Gogh, or Pablo Picasso. In solitude, we seek ourselves. It's damn true, the existence of my soul doesn't mean we know them very well. To know your own soul, you have to go inside. When you can't go outside, you should go inside. Solely & with solitude, these artists get lost into the process deeply and come out as a new soul because when they feel lost, they don't feel they are outside but inside and when we know ourselves, that's the best satisfaction in the world. They become fire, and aroused with what they do, even more than doing intense sex. For solitude, ***Georgia Okeeffe acquired a property in the Ghost Ranch area***, most precisely in Abiquin, New Mexico. She loved the area because it's was near the desert landscape. In 1942, she stated, ***'Such a beautiful untouched lonely feeling place, such a fine part of what I call the 'faraway'.'***

- Okay, this is damn necessary but avoided by most people; to remain unique. ***Unique people are different and sometimes out of the box.*** If you are out of the box then you have to live outside, all alone but with passing f time, such people call themselves Aliens because they have unique style. People usually love their style but they don't get accepted in society easily. When you speak the truth, you destroy the lies of society, so why society would like you. Nikola Tesla felt this every moment in his lifetime but I feel, that's the power. If you were born to stand out, then why to stand in. Just sharpen yourself and be the right one. *Create the most stunning, visually powerful and emotionally involved masterpieces.*

- In ancient times, when people had nothing to do, art was their sole choice & due to extreme details, competence & strength, even the great artist got failed but they all were best in their times & the interesting fact is, people still had enough time to look at the details even while creating them. Being busy is always a challenge for every generation and everyone wants to be busy with what they love. *What could be better than doing what you want to do?* To create details, you have to be idle, doing nothing and focus on nature, that's it, that's the key to create the best artworks of all time.

To impress an artist, be his art.

Strategy 28

SUPERHUMAN: The Absolute Blessings of Going with The Gold of Nature - Staying Active – A Japanese Proverb

Purpose of the Strategy: The impact of staying active in your work - How to become a superhuman just by following the rules of Nature.

Only staying active will make you want to live a hundred years. - A Japanese Proverb.

Why we are fascinated by Japanese culture! because they are more active than most individuals in the world in both personal and professional lives. You know, Japanese people have the longest life expectancy in the world even though they are highly active in professional life too. *It's astounding to know; life expectancy of Japanese males is 81.05 years while 87.09 for females and this data was collected in 2023.* This data is enough to make us curious to know why they are so highly active along with getting busy and making time for things. Their longevity has a direct connection with their productivity. *The level of your obsession is purely dependent on how alert you are while doing your work.*

Lao Tzu articulated some genius words, 'Nature doesn't hurry yet everything is accomplished.' We feel, we are most comfortable in accomplishing our best work when we go with the rules of nature instead of going against it. When we oppose something, we need double force and that can make anyone mad in the long run. It's easy to go with the flow when the flow is absolute truth. So, why we can't take the help of the best time and make our productivity double even without more efforts. I mean, that's incredibly smart. You don't have to oppose yet you will do the best of your life without hampering your health. That's brilliant. Hence, what makes me so surprised while observing the Japanese culture; simplicity and minimalism. While modernisation is pushing us to do more work in adverse times, Japanese people do the right work at the right time when they get the right energy. I mean, you can be hyper productive while opposing nature in the short run but you will destroy your potential and health in the long run, so what would be the use of your destination if the journey is painful. It's enjoyable to reach destination when journey is good otherwise the exhausted journey can make your destination worst. Remember that. So, masterpieces are often created in nature or by going with the flow of nature.

Japanese people stay active in everything but how and what they really do! We have done in-depth research which will guide you forever:

- *The first thing we realise in Japanese culture are their bright mornings.* They have the crisp to wake up with a bright smile and curiosity that you would jump out of bed. They don't hurry in the morning for their work even if they are workaholics and that makes them ready for the entire day by saving tremendous energy. They sip their morning drink like green or flowers tea along with their loved ones. That's the secret. They follow the norms of nature. *First,* they drink green tea that works as a detoxification agent and then becoming social instead of just running for work. We all are social animals and we need talking, sharing our emotions and ideas because we are made like that. We have to do it happily. That's the rule of nature. It's simple yet most people in the obsession of work, keep aside everything and wonder why they aren't happy. Social interaction is the primary need of humans. Remember that. They even feel the silence with their loved ones which is very brilliant. Also, the rule of socializing came from stone age people. These people were usually organised into groups and were highly socialized with the aim of surviving.

- *Second, when the entire world is sleeping on the bed, following the rules of modernisation, they are still sleeping on a traditional bed called a futon.* Futon are thin padded mattresses which can be laid directly on the floor but these mattresses aren't easy to sleep on as you may feel like you are sleeping on the floor and can cause joint pain. If possible, try to spend most of your time on the floor as when we sit, we absorb direct energy from it.

- ***Now, it's no wonder, Japanese people have the healthiest diet in the world.*** They enjoy calm mornings along with their green tea, not the milk tea. Their diet is mostly combined with a lot of vegetables and fruits and they eat meals many times a day in small qualities that give them proper time to digest those small quantities and keep them healthy. It's damn true, when we eat healthy food, it makes us super active and encourages you to do more work and that's what they are doing. They usually go with the seasonal diet and do frequent exercise along with it. Also, they laugh a lot to stay healthy. No matter how busy you are, don't ignore your social circle.

- ***Japanese people encourage the entire world to focus on cleanliness and hygiene.*** Shuzaburo Kagiyama stated, 'I have seen thousands of people cleaning toilets; without exception, everyone becomes humble when they clean the toilets. And your humbleness is reflected in your work relationships. They say when they clean the toilets, it purifies the mind, brings good luck and changes your fortune.'

- Nature tells us to feel the moment. ***Japanese people follow the rule of mindfulness.*** It says to be present in the moment which will improve your focus and enjoyment. They embrace imperfection, have gratitude and eat in moderation at 80% capacity.

- ***Above all, the rule of nature suggests us to sleep on time.*** Nature doesn't hurry yet everything is accomplished. Japanese people wake up early, take proper reasonable naps in between and sleep on time and yet they are the most productive people in the world. It reflects their attitude to work on their own self every moment and don't paying attention to bullshit & staying grateful for what they have. They really have the napping technique in their work culture which is very common. They fight with exhaustion by taking naps. In their work culture, most companies have nap rooms for employees to sharpen their focus and productivity while most culture focus on more work hours without giving rest to the employees but at end up, they become less productive even after doing work for long hours.

- We feel whatever you feel good, go with it. Go with nature, not against it. If you are super conscious of something good, apply the good instantly in your routine to make it a habit in your memory.

- ***Minimalism***, that's damn significant to declutter your mind. ***Japanese people aggressively follow minimalist style to stay away from what is not significant & carefully consider what is extremely close to their everyday moment.*** They even change and make it better for their everyday routine.

- Some random rules I love about Japanese culture is, ***they take warm bath at night which is known as Ofuno*** and this detoxifies their bodies and help in sleeping better. Also, Kaizen philosophy is much popular there. They do continuous slow improvements and reach a good state slowly even without much efforts. They are polite, respectful & always on time. The most significant thing that negatively changed us from the stone age to our advanced homo sapiens stage is our social connections. Earlier, we were dependent & working together for food and shelter but now we are growing all alone by our own choice; a drastic change in human history. Stone Age people were highly active that's why they discovered fire, wheels, containers, clothing, used bones for tools and carved rock and made paintings.

- The Power of Nature signifies to improve the four human factors i.e. Physical, Mental, Emotional, and Spiritual. Let dig into each term separately:

A. Physical: *Put your health first even before your work, go for regular walks to stay active, eat healthy food and be super conscious of what you are eating, always sleep on time and always take less stress and work more. Take more action.*

B. Mental: *To improve yourself mentally, read more books, update yourself with the great ideas, be curious and passionate, listen to great music, & limit your mind from the people who distract you. Don't fear to rise if you are the only one.*

C. Emotional: *First, don't feed your ego to do the wrong deeds even in unconsciousness. Love more, expect less, accept more, don't hurt anyone, value relationships, & be passionate about love and life to dance forever in your life.*

D. Spiritual: *To become spiritually active, meditate regularly, take proper rest in between, take more & more pause if required but don't give up on your passion, always have positive attitude, love yourself too much and be kind to yourself and others.*

- I forgot to tell you one more thing, ***Japanese people make tea ceremonies in which they drink healthy teas and become socialized.*** They literally don't oppose nature. When we go along with nature, we have the best health, longevity, and great obsession with our work. Japanese people have discovered a concept called, ***Nagomi concept which was founded in 2003 by Norikatsu Hosoya of the Japan Pastel Hope Art Association (JPHAA).*** It is purely known as ***Pastel Nagomi***

Art which focuses on the creative process. First, the Nagomi concept focuses on a sense of ease, emotional balance, well-being and calmness. Nagomi art helps in relieving stress and unhappiness. The creative process helps in calming and puts a relaxing effect on the artists. *They say it's the process that matters, not the destination.*

- Also, ***they find harmony in diversity.*** They accept diverse things very well. Even if they are very successful, they stay low profile & stick to nature, no matter how much they have. They remain simple. It's damn true, in the sense of modernisation, we have forgotten nature's rules.

If you truly love nature, you will find beauty everywhere. - Vincent Van Gogh.

No masterpiece was ever created by a lazy artist. - Salvador Dali.

When nature has work to be done, she creates a genius to do it. - Ralph Waldo Emerson.

Only simplicity can solve complexity.

Strategy 29

What If Today Is the Last Day of Our Lives!

I never imagined that so many days would ultimately make such a small life. - Franz Kafka.

Karl Marx voiced the most brilliant last words; 'Last words are for those fools who haven't said enough.' Humankind is always confused between whether to live for today or save something for the future. Why do people try so hard to win everything in life even if everything would get vanished with their last breath! They wouldn't even remember anything. What's the point of doing the best when at the end everyone would die! When my mother was suffering from cancer and still fit and fine, she was shifted to the palliative care unit where most last stage cancer patients were kept to give them the best treatment. When I saw my mother, she was extremely active and I realised most patients in that ward was counting their last days, still the doctors and nurses were taking care of them as they would live forever. They were taking care of their every need which were creating immense happiness for them. Affirmative, even in the last few days, to make them happy, doctors were trying their best. That's the pure reason for life. To live your everyday as a last day because when the last day comes, you will not realise whether it's really your last day or not. Just after a week, my mother died as gallbladder cancer spread into his entire nervous system. Are you feeling afraid after reading this? But that's the bitter reality of life and people realise this too late. ***Why was Pablo Picasso painting on his last day?*** Because he loved it. Even for a moment, we all want to die with a great feeling that we have done something in our lives and for that, we try to do anything, some try to build wealth, some self-satisfaction, some help people while some build good relationships but at the end we all want someone to take care of us. I know, why I'm explaining it all in this book because that's extremely significant. Do you want to take your last breath fearlessly? Of course, we all want to. We are all fearless just realising we have enough time to overcome our fears but trust me, we really don't have.

I have heard many real tales of people who were dying of cancer and regretting the things they wanted to do but never did. They missed the time in their own fear, regrets, sorrow and other people's opinions but they realised the lack of time had killed all their fear or a sense of rejection. In their last time, they wanted to fly high but they couldn't. The right time to overcome your fear is when you have enough time so you can live the rest of your life as you want. It's truly the time that brings fear & those who live in the present, live better and are ready to die anytime. ***So, if you feel like you have enough time, then you are challenging god.*** We recommend you to be highly obsessed with what you love, so anytime when you face death, you can say you were already living well. Live in this moment and tomorrow will take care of itself.

Do you know about the last three wishes of Alexander the Great? When Alexander was dying and all the best doctors were unable to treat him, he realised his **first wish;** the best doctors would carry his coffin to make people realise that even the best doctors couldn't save him. Also, his **second wish** depicted that the wealth he had accumulated including money, gold, or precious stones should be scattered in the way of procession to the cemetery and **third wish** clarified that his hands should be left loose, hanging outside the coffin to make people see, even after winning the entire world, he's going empty handed. We feel, the purpose of life isn't what you get but how you feel about yourself and what you make others feel; how well you were satisfied with what you were doing. What people actually desire, to live their last breath with love & with something they truly love.

- ***Today is the best day and today can be our last day.*** Let's do what we truly love from our hearts, so when death approaches us, we don't beg for it to come back after a few days. There are no last wishes, only last days.

- Fear is stupid. It takes courage to take risks. Most people realise this fact in their last days.

- ***Ludwig Wittgenstein stated, 'Death is not an event in life; we do not live to experience death. If we take eternity to mean not infinite temporal duration but timelessness, then eternal life belongs to those who live in the presence.'***

- ***And in the end, only the beauty of life matters.*** How beautiful life is, or how miserable it is, live in between. Today is the best day. Tomorrow is an illusion. It may come or not.

Today is happening and the past is gone. Try doing your best today. If yesterday was painful, think of today's smile. If you can smile right now, you are winning my friend. Never stop working on what you really love even on your last day.

- *If today is the last day of my life, I would love to live time with her in a sunflower garden, chasing the sun in that chilling winter, eating berries, writing a few poems for you & at last, I would die on her chest.*

- **Many people don't know Pablo Picasso worked until his last moment. On April 8th, he was working until 3am which was just hours before his death.**

- Ralph Waldo Emerson voiced, 'Write it on your heart that every day is the best day of the year.'

- If you feared death, it would come. If you feared life, it wouldn't.

- I really love this quote from Marcus Aurelius, 'Think of yourself as dead. You have lived your life. Now take what's left and live it properly.'

We should all start to live before we get too old. - Merilyn Monroe.

Do not fear death, live fully & leave a legacy. - Plato.

Only put off until tomorrow what you are willing to die having left undone. - Pablo Picasso.

Strategy 30

Epilogue: If You Love A Cactus, It's No Longer A Cactus - A Life Changing Strategy!

What keeps my heart awake is colourful silence. - Claude Monet.

Why does history remember artists for too long? Because artists love and, in love, everything becomes easy. When you are in love, you can make anything so easy that you would be able to do your best or even the world's best and you would get the best feeling, not because you have done the world's best but because you did it while loving it. In deserts, cacti aren't appreciated by all but what difference would it make. Even if you don't love them, cacti would remain the same in the desert and may be their intensity increases with time too. So, when you can't change something, you aren't allowed to hate it. It's the part of life & nature. For the epilogue I chose the above said subtitle because we all aren't fortunate to do what we want but sometimes we are forced to do what we truly hate and still we have to do it. Hence, when we love a cactus, it's no longer a cactus. *When you stop opposing what you hate, you will get time to know and maybe you will love it later.* I still feel; this is the best lesson of my life. I don't have much power over this life every time, so I should understand things as well as my enemies deeply. When you start loving everything, everything will change around you. You will dance like a mad person. Love is extremely easy when you are truly in it. ***Claude Monet stated, 'Every day I discover more and more beautiful things. It's enough to drive one mad. I have such a desire to do everything, my head is bursting out.'*** We feel, in love, most artists find a true life. Make your true emotions your life, so you don't have to chase for what we truly love.

We have observed all the obsessed artists of this world and we found, all were the true lovers of nature. Nature has diversity and its absolute truth. Ralph Waldo Emerson explained, 'The earth laughs in flowers.' If you want to understand God, understand what he made. Even though Claude Monet said, ***'My wish is to stay always like this, living quietly in a corner of nature.'*** Madness in life is given to the fortunate people because in insanity we find sanity at the end. Edgar Allan Poe explained, 'Men have called me mad; but the question is not yet settled, whether madness is or is not the loftier intelligence.'

- ***To live forever, choose everyday as a moment and forever too.*** To live the entire day in a moment is like feeling the pleasure of eternity.

- To be an artist, you have to wonder naturally & honestly and find what astonishes you. So, day by day, you will create yourself before this world. When you find what you truly love, you would learn the value of every second to invest in it madly.

- Anytime you try to do something with your heart, do it solely and in silence. *I learned, when we watch TV along with food, we pay attention to the TV, not the taste.*

- *Put hard sweat in the work even if you don't get results because if you are doing what you love, you are already winning.* Meanwhile you would become the best person with time and win eventually. So, at the end, you will win when you love honestly.

- Miracles do happen but after hard work in the right direction.

- *If you love a cactus it's no longer a cactus. The pain isn't in the injury but in the intensity and intensity increases when we hate something. When you love something, you would rarely feel pain from it.*

- Surround yourself with what makes you peaceful, not happiness. We become peaceful with our heart, not with our intelligence. Focus on making and investing in your emotions in the right place. Even with great intelligence, good work can fail you because you may feel like you are draining your soul.

Miscellaneous Tips & Tricks to Increase the Intensity of Obsession with Your Loving Work. Basically, it's a kind of summary:

- We can become successful in the tasks we don't care about its success because that's how it we do our best from our heart, not just to reach any level to by someone.

- Remember, interesting people can live alone who know how to occupy themselves intelligently without human connection.

- If you want to stand out, speak the universal truth. You don't need to be a master or famous but to find the right things only & everything will fall into your space.

- Don't get obsessed about the outcome but process. A great process always leads to great outcomes. In addition, don't get too obsessed because when sometimes obsession is not controlled, it may become dangerous.

- Walking increases the mind's interaction with the environment so, always take a long walk to generate ideas.

- I have learned this deep lesson from the artists. The best way to live a great life is to do what we really love & get extremely obsessed with it. The key to focus is where you don't have to live the entire time.

- Maybe your weirdness is your quality to make yourself stand out. Keep finding yourself.

- This world is insisting on making everything arduous but the key to a happy and disciplined living is to become simplest in the entire universe & to perceive everything simple.

- The more you enjoy your art, the better you would focus & ultimately the best artworks of your life.

- The same task is difficult when you are in pain as compared to when you are happy. A happy man does more than a sad man can ever do. Be happy or choose what makes you happy and peaceful.

- As an artist, my only suggestion is to slow down when you want to speed up otherwise you will lose the pleasure of creating your art. Slow down to focus on the details. Your best work is yet a few steps away.

- I got unhappy when I didn't get what I wanted but then I realized, did I get happy when I got what I desired for the entire life. Stay grateful.

- Do not give what customers want but serve them with what they mostly need because customers usually want something different but need something else. Fulfil their need.

- ***Steve Jobs is well known as a perfectionist*** so, don't ever tell anyone that perfection don't exist. Apple founder Steve Jobs paid extreme attention to the details. He was known as a frame fucker as we mentioned.

- Always be direct or blunt about what doesn't match your standards otherwise you will have to go down to reach them. That's look aggressive but the best part.

- Your energy goes to everybody; make sure it's magnetic & high. People want to be around high energetic and happy people.

- ***To solve complex problems, simplify and go into the details. Simplicity is the key to mass success. Think clear.***

- Don't make products that you have to promote. Make such products that make people uneasy and enforce them to steal from you. A great product has no price. Marketing is overrated. Don't ever beg in front of the customer to buy your product. Make something they need & want & you will never ever have to do any marketing in life.

- ***Life is short and long at the same time. Do it now or you will regret it later, for not the mistakes but for not trying.*** Birth & Death are the absolute truth & there's pure evidence that nothing gold would ever stay in our lives except the experience. Enhance your experience. Stay stupid. Stay fearless. Live your life.

- Focus on your diet strictly. Focus on fruits, seeds, & ultimately a healthy diet to make yourself feel great.

- Motivation is the biggest enemy because the things that are motivating you today will become demotivation is the adverse times. Be ruthless & merciless with your passion & follow it greatly.

- ***Steve Jobs depicted, 'Exercise clean thinking, simplify and ask yourself what is the core objective.'***

- Be alert, if you want to take control of your super conscious. While writing this book, I learned a lot about myself & my passion and understood, 'Be super conscious if you want to control and lead your life. Time is valuable, not money. For a true goal enthusiast, time is more significant than money and the same goes for artists.

- ***Passionate people have music in their minds & they don't stop dancing even if the entire world gets on fire.***

- We get more exhausted by not taking action than by doing the hardest task of this world. Be alert and take action to transform your life.

- ***Elon Musk sounded, 'Trying to be useful. You only become successful when you add value to society.'***

- Most people usually try to cut out their sleep and stay awake more to do more work but even after they shorten their sleep cycle to accomplish more work, they won't necessarily get more work done due to less focus & productivity.

- If you want best output of your work, do intense work or leave because you may waste your precious time.

- Reading is significant because it's the same direction journey. You create focus along with time. It helps in learning more and improves our imagination.

- Money is never the goal for passionate people but people mostly perceive their money only. The journey they once started because of their strong goals.

- It's a short tip; if you feel like your mind is heavy, stop working, take a pause, rest & live some time with yourself & you will be fine again.

- Never eat a meal just before you sleep. Also, never use phone before you sleep and instantly after waking up in the morning.

- ***Walt Disney*** *elaborated, 'All the adversity I've had in my life, all the troubles and obstacles, I have strengthened me. You may not realise it when it happens, but a kick in the teeth may be the best thing in the world for you.' Also,* **Jack Canfield** *stated, 'Don't worry about failures, worry about the chances you miss when you don't even try.'*

- You get 100% failed already when you halt your steps with fear. My friend, a step with courage is a partial failure but a partial success too. Keep moving forward.

- Do you believe humans are selfish? Diogenes lived an honest life and he was truly a cynic. A cynic is someone who believes that humans are selfish and that they only do something if it will benefit themselves. It even criticizes an act of kindness & will probably tease if you help someone, just because you want some relief by helping somebody. So, you can sleep better at night. What do you think?

- History glorifies, one day Diogenes begged for money from a statue, and when asked why he was doing so, replied, 'I'm getting practice to being refused.'

- Don't look for more but enjoy in less. Find more and create more within. They key is to go inside. Focus is life.

- Now, here comes the masterpiece of Diogenes. ***When people asked on how Diogenes wished to be buried,*** *he left instructions to be thrown outside the city wall so that wild animals could feast on his body. When asked if he minded this, he said, Not at all, as long as you provide me with a stick to chase the creatures away.' and when asked how he could use the stick as he was dead and people scolded him that he lacked awareness on how he could use a stick if he was dead and for that he replied, If I lack awareness, then why should I care what happens to me when I'm dead? He made fun of people's excessive concern with the proper treatment of the dead.*

- That's damn dark, in this internet generation, we all are quoting, so we can find alike people & seek discomfort even in the discomfort. Mass gives us courage even if it's wrong.

- Alexander the Great said some heart wrenching last words, 'A tomb now suffices for him for whom the world was not enough.'

- You are what you think about yourself. If you think you are good, you will reach towards it by changing yourself. You think you are the world's best person and one day you will be.

- The more focused you are while carrying out your work, the longer you will remember it whether it's loving someone or your skills. Live from inside to outside for forever happiness.

- Energy is Genius. People are attracted to our energy and character, not our intelligence.

- I don't know who said this but this is brilliant, 'Work in a way that makes you proud of the result.'

- How to become people's magnet! Make people extremely happy, enjoy, laughable and peaceful in your presence and they will ring your bell every day!

- Haruki Murakami sounded, 'I can bear any pain as long as it has meaning.'

- If you are a true artist & creating something, go for your 100% then go for 500% and then go for extreme infinity and intensity that you would make it almost close to perfect and find the absolute truth during the process.

- Bill Gates clarified, 'If you are born poor it's not your mistake, but if you die poor, it's your mistake.' He also said, 'To win big, you sometimes have to take big risks.' Also, 'If your business is not on the internet, then your business will be out of business.'

- Just like ignorance of law is no excuse, likewise ignorance of consciousness and awareness is no excuse. You have to work on yourself honestly.

- You know, Bill Gates had a goal for himself to become a billionaire with his company before he reached 30 years of his age. Always set a goal to give your mind a direction, speed and intensity.

- Everything is non-sense if you aren't curious.

- Adapt the change or become neutral to the change. Stephen Hawking suggested, *'Intelligence is the ability to change.'* We found, it's your ability that makes all the difference. It's not your IQ but your attitude that makes you into the person you want to become. His last words were, 'There is no heaven. It's a fairy story.' He also explained in an interview with New York Times 'While living, my expectations were reduced to zero when I turned 21. Everything since then has been a bonus.'

- I have finally cracked it. We don't want to say more words but expressing our emotions. That's why words aren't enough when we are glad & gloomy.

- I hope you are reading and understanding this book but kindly be aware, a writer is always found between the words. Franz Kafka stated, 'Everything that you love, you will eventually lose, but in the end, love will return in a different form.'

- You can go without anything but can't go without the work you love the most. You would feel like something is missing. Work makes our life satisfied. It's the most significant part of our lives. Always target the most loving work as soon as you get the energy.

- An artist never misses the details, never ever. It's how these details make him a true artist; that's the true process; that's how the spectators get astonished; that's how an artist feels satisfied when he finds out everything in between & that's what a true love of an artist is.

- Love is underrated and comes irregularly but it's most essential and needed every moment.

- ***Vincent Van Gogh depicted, 'I am always doing what I cannot do yet, in order to learn how to do it.'***

- I'm really fascinated by ancient history. This gives me vibes & makes to forget myself into any time dimension. May be that's time travel.

- Alfred Hitchcock mostly called as the master of suspense as he had the art to create better films even in a room that could bring the audience to the edge of their seats. He described, 'To make a great film, you need three things - the script, the script, and the script.'

- *If you can't entertain yourself when you are alone, you really have a long way to go ahead in this life.*

- The man who makes everything that leads to happiness depends upon himself, and not upon another man, has adopted the very best plan for living happily. - Plato, the republic.

- Michael Jackson suggested, 'Study the greats and become greater. Don't be afraid to be different.' We feel, save your time for the first discovery, till tell learn from the greats.

- Throughout humankind history, people who were truly artistic, never felt alone. God is a great artist who created humans who also love art for their lives. This is a genius work. *Socrates said, 'Wonder is the feeling of a philosopher and philosophy begins in wonder.' Also, he voiced, 'It is better to change an opinion than to persist in the wrong one.*

- We have learned; when we don't get satisfaction in our work, we try to find it somewhere else and then more places and it becomes a habit. We would never get satisfied until we are dependent on external elements for our happiness & satisfaction. The more I know myself, the more I understand the control of events I don't have.

Recently, I found a 'Before I die' project on the internet where people are sharing their 'Before I Die Dreams' and I found some which were enchanting, gorgeous & heart wrenching at the same time:

A. Before I die, I want to wake up early.

B. Before I die, I want to be myself around others.

C. Before I die, I want to repair my broken heart.

D. Before I die, I want to be brave on the road less travelled.

E. Before I die, I will abandon all insecurities.

F. Before I die, I want to be someone's favourite.

The more I think it's over, the more I feel that there is nothing more truly artistic than to love people. - Vincent Van Gogh.

Pleasure & action make the hours seem short. - William Shakespeare.

From my rotting body, flowers shall grow and I am in them, and that is eternity. - Edvard Munch.

I'm living well while seeking something I love but still far away, maybe reaching, or maybe extremely close to it.

About the Author

Deepak Gupta stands as a distinguished author renowned for his ability to craft accessible, meticulous, and pragmatic self-help literature. With an impressive extensive portfolio comprising over *forty titles*, his work transcends mere words, leaving a lasting mark on readers seeking guidance and inspiration, including the distinguished "*10 Principles to Beat Failure*," which not only secured the prestigious *Google Best Choice 2018 award but also attained the status of a Top Seller on Google Play Store in 2019.*

His lauded "*30 Minutes Read & 10 Principles Series*" has garnered widespread acclaim, amassing over 1 million readers worldwide and earning appreciation from diverse corners of the globe. Rooted in a philosophy of extracting and embodying exceptional content from his subconscious mind, Gupta's work delves into a numerous topic, ranging from social issues to inspirational truths, encapsulated in compelling short stories and heart-warming poetry. Also, he has garnered significant readership with his acclaimed books, notably including "10 Principles to Beat Failure," "The Rules of being Highly Productive," "10 Principles to Love Yourself," and "The Girl with No Dreams." Among these, "*The Girl with No Dreams*" *stands out as a cherished fantasy short tale, appreciated for its captivating narrative and a uniquely twisted ending that has resonated deeply with readers.*

The author's dedication to authenticity is reflected in his extensive travels across India, exploring locales such as Manali, Rajasthan, Goa, Kolkata, Madhya Pradesh, Jammu, Dalhousie, Mussoorie and more. These experiences infuse his work with a genuine and unique perspective, capturing the essence of diverse cultures and landscapes.

Deepak Gupta's academic journey includes earning a post-graduation degree from the prestigious *Delhi School of Economics*, underscoring the intellectual depth that permeates his literary creations.

Beyond the realm of literature, Gupta finds solace and inspiration in his exquisite terrace garden, a testament to his appreciation for beauty and serenity. Residing in Delhi, India, he shares his life with his family, embodying the principles he imparts in his writings.

As a prolific author, Deepak Gupta continues to release new books every month, with the aim of fostering a profound connection between readers and the universal truths that define the human experience. *His professional acumen, coupled with a genuine passion for delivering life-enriching insights, make him distinguished.*

Keep in touch with Deepak via the web:
Instagram @authordeepakgupta
Facebook: facebook.com/authordeepakgupta
Twitter @authordeepakgup
E-mail: guptadeepak3111994@gmail.com

Don't miss out!

Visit the website below and you can sign up to receive emails whenever Deepak Gupta publishes a new book. There's no charge and no obligation.

https://books2read.com/r/B-A-AQXE-THXZC

BOOKS 2 READ

Connecting independent readers to independent writers.

Did you love *Irresistible Obsession*? Then you should read *10 Principles to Live Peacefully*[1] by Deepak Gupta!

The real enlightenment of humans is not by avoiding or escaping life, but through it, gracefully.

You know, the God is connected with emotions and hope, but humans are connected with mind and intelligence. *In any century, most of the intelligent people have been failing to grasp the secret to become peaceful all the time.* Predominantly when we need mental stabilization, we fail to find something meaningful in our intelligence. Most humans change in life when they experience pain. We don't essentially change with

1. https://books2read.com/u/bWE5eW

2. https://books2read.com/u/bWE5eW

minds but with emotions. We are the creatures of emotions and that's why we get distressed in our lives even how much intelligent and educated we are. *Moreover, our generation is embracing to find solutions in deep but mostly our answers are in the simple aspects of life. When the extraordinary man understands the ordinary man, the distinction starts ending.*

People aren't hopeless. They think they are hopeless. As a whole, we aren't downhearted; we are unaware of the happiness around ourselves.

Mental pain is less dramatic than physical pain, but it is more common and also hard to bear. - C.S. Lewis.

Read more at https://www.authordeepakgupta.com.

Also by Deepak Gupta

100 Minutes Read
Live Your Dream Life As You Want
God is a Great Philosopher

15 Minutes Read
Common Sense in the 21st Century

30 Minutes Read
How To Deal With Haters
One Second Rule: How to take Right Decisions quickly
without Thinking too Much
Hard Decisions Easy Life: Bandersnatch & The World of
Possibilities
Sell Your Talent: How to Convert Talent into Money along
with the Personality Development
Ideas & Origami
The Anti-Suicidal Self Help Book
The Therapy of Peace: Illustrated Edition

The Rules of Being Highly Productive
How to Think Everyday
Bedtime Thinker
The Rules of Being Highly Skillful
Blockchain Technology: The Future
Unlimited Human Potential
Kindness in Imperfect Life
Alas! The Boring Day
Hyperfocus Creativity
Marketing Mess
Slow to Fall in Love

Modern Classics
The Talkative Man
Santa on the Ground

Power
The Power of Universe
The Power of Nothing: They say and We do

Standalone
Inspiring Life
Zero Degree: An Icy Thriller
She: She Heals Everything
10 Principles To Beat Failure: Illustrated Enhanced Edition
Beta 2020

She's the Sunflower: Heart Healing Poetry and Prose

10 Principles To Love Yourself

How To Heal Yourself

She: She heals everything

Skyfall: Your Heart Will Fall Too

The Girl With No Dreams

The Pigeon With Broken Legs: Modern Classics Children Story

Average Mind: The World is not the Wonder. It's the Wonder which makes your World

Being Busy Is Not Always Productive: Stop Wasting your Time at the Wrong Place

Happiness Without Cause: Why Happiness was easy in the 19th Century but not in the 21st Century

Alone Than Lonely: How to Live Life without Attachment & Enjoy your Company

The Lost Child

The Power Pack of Short Stories: Box Set of Crime, Thriller & Suspense Stories

Earth 2200

Amazon Kindle & Google Play ebooks Pricing System: Maximize Your ebooks Sales

5 Principles To Dig Out Success

◇◇◇◇: Udhaar

The Little Book of Wise Quotes

But She Didn't Come

Deepak Gupta Collection: The Complete Self Help Book (2015-2020)

Revenge

Revolutionary Love: Friendship-Love-Revenge: A Novel

The Man Who Forgets

10 Principles to Live Peacefully
The Untold Life of My Sage Mother
Irresistible Obsession

Watch for more at https://www.authordeepakgupta.com.